Traces of Thoreau

Cape Cod Light · Truro

Traces of Thoreau

A Cape Cod Journey

Stephen Mulloney

NORTHEASTERN UNIVERSITY PRESS   BOSTON

Northeastern University Press

Library of Congress Cataloging-in-Publication Data
Mulloney, Stephen.
Traces of Thoreau : a Cape Cod journey / Stephen Mulloney.
p. cm.
Includes index.
ISBN 1-55553-344-2 (hardcover : alk. paper).—
ISBN 1-55553-343-4 (pbk. : alk. paper)
1. Cape Cod (Mass.)—Description and travel. 2. Thoreau,
Henry David, 1817–1862—Homes and haunts—Massachusetts—
Cape Cod. 3. Mulloney, Stephen—Journeys—
Massachusetts—Cape Cod. I. Title.
F72.C3M85 1998
917.44'92043—dc21   98-12874

Illustrations by Karol B. Wyckoff
Designed by Virginia Evans

Composed in Cochin by Coghill Composition, Richmond, Virginia. Printed
and bound by Thomson-Shore, Inc., Dexter, Michigan. The paper is
Glatfelter Supple Opaque Recycled, an acid-free sheet.

MANUFACTURED IN THE UNITED STATES OF AMERICA
02 01 00 99 98   5 4 3 2 1

To the memory of my father, Herbert, and my brother, James;
to my mother, Gladys, who kept the faith;
to Claire Kirby, whose gift got the whole thing started;
and to Donna, as promised

Hug the shore, let others keep to the deep.

VIRGIL, *Aeneid*

Minot

③ Marshfield

Plymouth

③

CAPE COD BAY

Race Point Provincetown Highland Light

Long Point Truro Ballston Beach

Newcomb Hollow

Wellfleet Cahoon Hollow

Le Count's Hollow

Marconi Beach

CAPE COD CANAL

Eastham Nauset Light

Coast Guard Beach

Sandwich 6A Brewster Orleans 28

Dennis

Bourne 6A Barnstable Yarmouth 6

28 Mashpee 6 Harwich Chatham

BUZZARDS BAY Hyannis 28

Falmouth 28 MONOMOY ISLAND

NANTUCKET SOUND

Acknowledgments

To start, I'd like to thank all the people of Northeastern University Press who helped turn a dream into reality: Director and Editor-in-Chief Bill Frohlich, Ann Twombly, Jill Bahcall, Tara Mantel, and Allison Morse. I'm especially grateful to the person who brought us together and made it all possible, my "shadow" agent, Northeastern University's government relations guru, Tom Keady.

Throughout the course of my project I was inspired by those who've gone before me and written about Cape Cod so lovingly and so well. Three of the best contemporary Cape-rooted writers took time out from their own busy book projects to read my manuscript, and I'm deeply indebted to the gracious, generous triad of William Martin, Greg O'Brien, and Robert Finch.

A few others of artistic bent spared some of their precious time to go over the manuscript, most notably my best friend, Richard Snee—Rocky, Rocky, how do you thank a man for a million laughs?—and his wife and fellow thespian, the dynamic Paula Plum. The artistic contributions to the book of my brother Robert Mulloney and my niece Jennifer Rattin are not visible to the naked eye, but they are indelibly etched in my heart.

Special thanks to Karol Wyckoff for her generous contribution of artwork; to Lois Pines for keeping my job open while I was on "sabbatical"; and to Frank Ackerman of the National Park Service. Frank has probably forgotten our long-ago interview, but I have not.

When I first went out to the beach I was a rank amateur as an ornithologist, but I have moved up in rank as a result of conversations I've had with naturalist Peter Trull, author of *A Guide to the Common Birds of Cape Cod*. My thanks to Peter, especially for his poking holes in the government's "blame it all on the gulls" philosophy of Monomoy Island wildlife management.

Finally, I doubt this book would have come about without the intercession of Francis de Sales, the patron saint of writers, and Saint Jude, who as always took care of the logistics.

I gratefully acknowledge Henry Holt and Company for permission to quote the following material:

The excerpt from "Devotion," by Robert Frost, from *The Poetry of Robert Frost*, edited by Edward Connery Latham, © 1956 by Robert Frost, copyright 1928, 1969 by Henry Holt and Company, Inc. Reprinted by permission of Henry Holt and Company, Inc.

From *The Outermost House* by Henry Beston, copyright 1928, 1956 by Henry Beston, © 1977 by Elizabeth C. Beston. Reprinted by permission of Henry Holt and Company, Inc.

Contents

Introduction

There are probably words addressed to our

condition exactly, which, if we could really

hear and understand, would be more

salutary than the morning or the spring to

our lives, and possibly put a new aspect on

the face of things for us. How many a man

has dated a new era in his life

from the reading of a book.

WALDEN

 It was a dark and stormy night, honest to God it was, that Ides of March eve of the fateful encounter. Sleet peppered the sitting room windows, raising such a racket that I could hardly hear myself think. Truth be told, it was a merciful distraction, for my thoughts matched the night in gloom and dissonance. The nasty weather had precluded my usual long, aimless walk with the dog, an evening constitutional that had become the high point of my day. Instead, grounded, restless, I roamed the house, room to room, which seemed to upset my intelligent, sensitive pup. With big, liquid eyes she looked up at me quizzically, as if to say, "Tell me what's wrong, so I can help."

It had been a typically temperamental New England winter all around: January vicious, thawless, February a false spring, and then March, in like a lamb, determined to go out like a lion. Daylight was supposed to be lengthening, but I found myself needing to snap on the lamps by 2:00 each murky afternoon. When the temperature rose above freezing it snowed, while more than one bitterly cold night had been disturbed by the rumble of thunder and the flash of lightning. I wouldn't have been half surprised to catch the sun rising in the west and setting in the east, if in fact that supreme luminary ever decided to show its face again.

Sources of my malaise and unease that March night were general (no doubt I was suffering from an acute case of seasonal affective disorder) as well as specific: I was anxiously waiting to hear if I'd been accepted into the graduate program at Harvard's Kennedy School of Government. But each dreary day's mail brought no telltale thick envelope with a Cambridge postmark, only *billets doux* from my legion of creditors.

I'd put all my eggs in the Kennedy School basket, seeing it as the last best hope to jump-start my career and catch up with my friends, every last one of whom was flourishing. The years were going by "fast as snowflakes," but both my personal and professional lives had seemingly stalled as the final decade of the millennium counted down its second year.

Lives of quiet desperation unfold differently (not to mention indifferently), I suppose, with no two tales alike except, perhaps, for a common pathos. In a nutshell, my story was this: approaching forty, I was recently out of a job as a television reporter on Cape Cod, laid off thanks to the region's faltering economy. What's worse, I was also out of a Cape romance, pinkslipped from love's labor for reasons I was still trying to figure out. Now I was doing some freelance reporting (read: "between jobs"), living back home in Boston with my mother.

"Never complain, never explain," said Henry Ford. Well, he was half right. I often felt compelled to explain to people (especially women I was dating) why I was "at home" pushing middle age. It was mostly a matter of finances: the death of my father a few years earlier, followed by the stunning death of my brother little over a year after that, had wreaked havoc on a small family business concern and nearly pushed us into insolvency. I moved in with my mother to help her pay off a refinanced mortgage so that she could stay secure in the home she loved. You've got to do the right thing. In the meantime I mightily resisted being cast as the stereotypical aging Irish Catholic bachelor, a trite and threadbare image that was at odds with my true persona, even if I met the key criteria. I was no Cliff Clavin, the hapless mama's boy from *Cheers*; no, in my mind I was more like Frank Capra's *mensch* George Bailey, just lacking someone to play Donna Reed's part, and still waiting for a guardian angel to come along and show me my wonderful life.

Unable to take the dog out that night of storm and stress, bored near to tears, I searched for a book to read, any book. It wasn't an easy task; I'd read almost everything on the shelves at least twice. Suddenly I came across a bag containing a gift from a friend, who'd recently rummaged through a second-hand bookstore and put together a care package for me. I reached in and pulled out the first volume, an old hardcover that nearly came apart in my hands. It was *Cape Cod,* by Henry David Thoreau, an account of his walking tours on the peninsula during the 1840s and 1850s. My first reaction was, "Oh, no, not *that* old fart."

I can't recall whether I thumbed through Thoreau during college; I may have merely read the Cliffs Notes. Many of my peers admired *Walden* and Thoreau's writing on civil disobedience, but I'd heard that the author was a sour curmudgeon and so avoided his works; I'd had enough live curmudgeons to deal with. And if I had wanted to read about the Cape that miserable evening, I would have preferred to curl up with a recently published bestseller also titled *Cape Cod,* a mystery by William Martin. Given the prevailing mood, dour Mr. Thoreau seemed an unappealing choice.

Nevertheless, out of sheer curiosity I started reading the book anyway. To my surprise, it gripped me immediately. In fact, it turned out to be a real page turner, and I kept with it past bedtime. By the time I finished it was dawn, and another weary late winter day was poking its pasty face in my window. I should have been exhausted, but instead I felt more alive than I could remember.

Cape Cod sent pangs of warm delight shooting through me, analogous to the feeling you get when you stumble across a treasured memento long misplaced and given up for lost. The words and experiences of the footloose nineteenth-century intellectual had stimulated my cerebrum, broken my chronic cabin fever, roused a slumbering wanderlust; I knew I needed to get a life, and it was as if Thoreau had shouted at me from the pages: "This way!"

The book touched me in other ways not yet definable, though this much was certain: by first light I felt myself free of a dread "three o'clock in the morning in the soul" feeling that had haunted me these past few months—indeed, these past few years. This

was a most salutary and welcome dividend, and through the intercession of a most unlikely Samaritan I'd gained a fresh purpose
for going on. Up from vaults of despair sprang images of a life
remastered, revived and restored to its original promise, brightened and freshly colored by ideas and possibilities. I could envi-
sion myself among the living again, walking, writing. From the
reading of a book a new era had dawned, I felt sure of it.

Although I expected Thoreau's prose to be stilted and old-
fashioned, aside from a few words such as "perchance" and "methinks," I found it to be "completely modern," as Henry Beston
noted in my edition's introduction. I especially appreciated the
book's conversational tone and the author's unexpected sense of
humor, which had me reevaluating the curmudgeon image. Later
I would read how critics have rolled their eyes at Thoreau's at-
tempts to elicit laughs (Paul Theroux calls them "groaners"), but
they were quite to my taste—I happen to enjoy puns, and you've
got to admire a guy who was telling lawyer jokes a century and a
half ago, to wit: "Until quite recently there was no regular lawyer
below Orleans. Who then will complain of a few regular man-
eating sharks along the backside?"

The Cape Cod described by Thoreau is in many ways unrecog-
nizable to those who know it now. In the mid-1800s, the thinly
populated, inhospitable peninsula was a sandy wasteland owing
to wholesale deforestation, having "such a surface, perhaps, as
the bottom of the sea made dry land day before yesterday." Still,
I was thrilled to come across mention of some points of interest
that I myself had observed. For instance, Thoreau tells how a
sudden drop in temperature sent boat passengers scrambling for
coats within sight of sweltering Provincetown. I myself had experienced this rapid sea change in the air off Provincetown on even
the hottest days; it remains a chilling summer phenomenon, one

well known to patrons of the Bay State Line's Boston–Cape Cod ferry.

But it was Thoreau's description of what he calls the Cape's "backbone," the high bank on the Atlantic shore extending from Eastham to Highland Light in Truro, that really grabbed my attention. Although this geologic formation has existed since the last Ice Age, I was quite taken by the fact that Thoreau and I had both laid eyes on it and come away equally impressed. From that point on, he was no longer a distant figure mounted on history's pedestal—our mutual perception of the sea cliff helped telescope the gap in time between us, drawing me closer to the flesh-and-blood Thoreau and the place where he had walked.

Reading the "backbone" passage, I recalled how I first came to appreciate the cliff's imposing majesty when on assignment years ago covering the story of a big New Bedford fishing boat gone aground on the "backside" by Wellfleet. That day I clambered down the bank, got a few interviews, had my photographer shoot some cover video, and then turned to leave. There, confronting me, stretching north and south as far as the eye could see, was an awesome sight, a huge unbroken earthen wall rising to heights of a hundred and fifty feet. Accustomed to looking down on this shore from scenic overlooks, for the first time I got a true view of the outer beach's magnificent composition.

Bound by monolithic cliff and sea, the great outer beach became the major focus of *Cape Cod*, and it was bound to become my focus as well. When he pondered the Cape's future, Thoreau rightly forecast that the Cape "must" eventually become a place of summer resort, but he also had a presentiment that its great outer beach might somehow remain unsullied. Although he probably couldn't ever have imagined that the United States government (with whom he was often at odds) would play the savior's role, the essential Cape Cod of Thoreau's book *has* been largely preserved and protected from development, through an act of Congress. Upon finishing *Cape Cod*, I knew I was destined to follow his footsteps, confident that I could share more of his experiences on what's now the Cape Cod National Seashore.

Intrigued by the strong, original voice that spoke to me from the pages of *Cape Cod*, I followed up by reading about Thoreau's life, some pertinent details of which served to cement a growing kinship I felt with the man. At heart a free spirit, Thoreau also lived with his mother on many occasions. His elder brother died at a relatively young age, as did mine, sudden passings that traumatized each of us respectively. Thoreau died a childless bachelor, and at the rate I was going, so would I. And for much of his life he was regarded as an ineffectual dreamer, a label (or less charitable variations thereon) that I suspect has been linked with my name once or twice in certain Boston salons.

Of course, there were significant differences between us other than our centuries, intellectual gifts, and accomplishments. Thoreau was a teetotaler, while I'm no stranger to the "bar-rooms of Massachusetts" he so disparaged. He also wrote, "I derive no pleasure from talking to a young woman half an hour simply because she has regular features." Would that I could make the same claim; if science could arrange it, I would gladly swap some of my testosterone for a portion of his brain matter.

But we came together on this central point: Thoreau wrote, "I did not see why I might not make a book on Cape Cod." Knowing of nothing that would cause me to hold back, I didn't see why I might not make a book on Cape Cod, too.

Cape Cod was the obvious inspiration for this volume's organization. Thoreau had noticed on a map that there's an unbroken stretch of Atlantic beach running from Eastham to Long Point,

Provincetown—not one single harbor, herring run, or tidal estuary in the way to impede forward progress. Thus "Cape Cod Beach"—the Great Beach, the backside, the outer beach—became his primary destination. In October 1849 he and a friend, William Ellery Channing, took public transportation overland to Orleans, followed the beach on foot thirty-odd miles to Provincetown, then returned to Boston by boat. Quite simply I planned to do the same, like Thoreau recording impressions as I went along, augmenting the account with historical tidbits or local color where appropriate.

I decided not to bed down at the exact spots Thoreau did, fearing that such an exercise might become stilted and predictable. Rather, I would adhere faithfully to his beach and dune route, but in the Thoreauvian spirit decided to opt for spontaneity when it came to "inland" encounters, so that my off-beach segments on the human side of Cape Cod would be thoroughly extemporaneous, as his were.

In all, the peripatetic Thoreau traversed the Cape four times, in 1849, 1850, 1855, and 1857. The 1849 walk (my model) provided him with *Cape Cod's* narrative frame, which he fleshed out with additional material gathered on the next two visits. (The 1857 trip, well detailed in his journal, was not a factor in the final book manuscript.) The number of visits is worth noting when you consider that few Americans in those days traveled strictly for pleasure or edification. Then as now the Cape's proximity and relative accessibility were great enticements—without having to go tremendous distances Thoreau found himself in another world, one very near unto itself, a consideration that appealed to him no less than it does to modern residents of the northeast megalopolis.

To the man from Concord, the Cape at first glance was a strange, alien place, and after placid Walden he found its wildness provocative. Almost from the start he was powerfully attracted to Cape Cod, and as his numerous sallies there attest, the region made a profound and lasting impression on him. When Thoreau described the storm-ravaged, ship-devouring coastline as "this voracious beach," he might also have been giving expression to the shore's other metaphoric appetites. As he himself discovered, and as countless others who have followed him would willingly affirm, Cape Cod can consume the human imagination as well.

Thoreau first saw the Cape when he was thirty-one. I on the other hand have had a lifelong relationship with Cape Cod, commencing even before I was born—my mother often walked Cape beaches while pregnant with me, and I know my inchoate heart captured their ocean rhythms as I floated in my own amniotic sea. I summered there as a child (the best years of my life, memory insists), spent my salad days sharing cramped vacation houses as a college student, and lived and worked year-round as a television reporter for the five years that the Cape was my beat. It is not without some justification that I claim more than a passing acquaintance with the place. Nevertheless, Thoreau's writings fired a desire to know the Cape even better, to take my awareness of its intrinsic nature to a more intimate level, to renew my appreciation of its *sui generis* geography.

After reading *Cape Cod,* I turned to the works of other regional writers. One, Henry Beston, opens his classic work *The Outermost House* with this riveting sentence: "East and ahead of the coast of North America, some thirty miles and more from the inner shores of Massachusetts, there stands in the open Atlantic the last fragment of an ancient and vanished land." Beston's bold description jarred me; absorbed with images of the contemporary Cape and all its modern connotations, I'd lost cognizance of just how dramatic the Cape's position in the world truly is, despite the fact that the outline of the "bared and bended arm" (to use Thoreau's words) was as familiar to me as my own features. It became clear that I must sharpen my viewpoint; in addition to gathering material for a book and indulging in a bit of meditative sabbatical, my goal was to look at Cape Cod anew, bringing to the task, I hoped, the kind of fresh vision the Argus-eyed Thoreau brought with him in 1849.

In the middle of planning this book, some good news arrived: I was accepted by the Kennedy School after all. Getting into Harvard meant a great deal to me; for one thing, it put me into a sort of fellowship with Thoreau, Harvard Class of 1837, and now I would feel less of a midget trying to walk in the great man's footsteps. No one can ever be completely at ease treading on the turf of Cape Cod's famous literary Henrys—Thoreau, Beston, and Kittredge—but as John Hay wrote of his own temerity in penning *The Great Beach*, "each to his own eye." Yes, and to his own foot.

I had put my trip to Cape Cod on hold while I was at school, but not for one minute did I forget that dark and stormy night, and what I had vowed to do. Three months after I received my degree I cleared the decks, swept aside petty obstacles, and was ready to go. It was Labor Day, and my objective was only a short bus ride away.

It had come time to venture east and ahead of North America!

Part One

Brewster Mill

KAROL B WYCKOFF

Labor Day

KAROL B. WYCKOFF

1

※ ※

East and Ahead

In autumn, even in August, the thoughtful

days begin, and we can walk

anywhere with profit.

———

CAPE COD

1. Busman's Holiday

 East and ahead! Well, south first. Then *east*. Then north, and finally west; such is the Cape's configuration that all points on the compass would be touched in the course of the coming excursion.

Waiting at Boston's South Station on a Saturday morning for the Plymouth & Brockton bus to the Cape, I noted with satisfaction that my trip was beginning in synch with the stars: the horoscope in the morning *Boston Globe* urged me and my fellow Leos to "get back to the earth for vitality." Having astrology in my corner, what more could I ask for? Coincidentally that same *Globe* edition also carried an op-ed piece penned by me under my current nom de plume, Senator ——— (I'd gone to work for the state legislature as a press secretary and ghostwriter). Publication and planetary benediction — such augers at journey's launch!

The bus filled quickly, and with all the window seats gone I ended up on the bench seat in back, next to the lavatory, which for the time being emitted a pleasant lemony scent. Idly I eyed my fellow holiday junketeers — a handful of youthful-looking seniors, a lot of twenty-somethings, one or two mothers with preadolescents, no babes in arms, no ancients. First arguable observation of the trip: men traveling casually prefer to wear jeans, whereas women opt for jogging suits.

Exceptions to the sartorial rule included a fellow in full hippie regalia (though he was of the Woodstock II generation), complete with shoulder-length hair, neck beads, sleeveless vest, and bell bottoms, as well as a young woman outfitted like a Dallas Cowboy cheerleader — white denim jacket, white short shorts, and white boots. If this were a scene from a movie, such anachronistic dress might be challenged by sticklers for detail, the type who get riled when they spot '47 Packards in World War II flicks, but in this case they would be off base. The retro looks were completely appropriate for the hand-me-down nineties, this vulgar *fin de siècle* marked by Broadway revivals, movies based on old TV shows, and oldies radio. What would be next, classic punk? O tempora! O mores! (Heading to find Thoreau's Cape Cod, your correspondent was not unaware of an element of irony in this pronouncement about our derivative culture.)

With a grating cough the bus kicked into action and backed out of its bay. I had felt a little stab of empathetic pain when one rider (the cowgirl) mentioned to the driver that she had to be at the Cape Cod Mall for work by 2:00 P.M.; many were the glorious summer days when I also had to report for duty, at the TV station or Hyannis saloon where I tended bar for extra cash, while the rest of the world was content to laze on the beach. This was the first time in recent memory that I was heading to Cape Cod *on vacation.*

We headed down the Southeast Expressway. At the old Keystone Building site, where the expressway veers sharply left, a splendid and unobstructed view of the southwesterly meandering Neponset River awaited. Ten minutes from downtown, five minutes from Dorchester's rough-and-tumble Fields Corner, a pastoral scene unfolded in surprising panorama: twisting river, marshland ceding to meadow beyond, all overlooked by a few grand homes set on sylvan heights. The landscape seemed barely changed from colonial times, when aristocrats took retreat from pestilential Boston at airy country estates in Milton. If I could paint the Neponset landscape, I'd title it *Tidewater Massachusetts.*

In short order the bus met up with Route 3 and barreled south, passing just west of seaside Hingham and Cohasset. In October 1849 Thoreau and Channing headed down that coastline by train when a huge storm delayed the boat they had planned to take from Boston to Provincetown. At Cohasset the pair came upon a victim of the storm, the brig *St. John* out of Galway, eviscerated by deadly rocks and shoals just offshore.

That day, the beach was littered with bodies of Irish immigrants in flight from the Great Famine, many coming to go "out to service" in Yankee families; nowadays, the very same South Shore is considered yet another "Irish Riviera," part of a vast Gaelic archipelago sprawled across the northeastern United States. From big fine houses on Cohasset's Jerusalem Road and Atlantic Avenue wealthy Irish-Americans, full-fledged members of a new elite, can drink in spectacular scenery, the ocean views encompassing an outcropping of rock known as the Grampuses, hard-hearted, unyielding granite that spelled doom for hundreds of their impoverished distant kin.

Norwell's woods held the first hint of fall color, but against an otherwise unrelenting sea of green the scattered yellowing bushes looked more like mutant or diseased specimens than harbingers of autumn. The bus rolled on to the North River, another Massachusetts waterway of historic import, along whose banks great sailing ships were built and which is purported to be the last unpolluted tidal river in Massachusetts. The North empties into Massachusetts Bay, and the point where river and ocean merge is among the most treacherous stretches on the entire coast. Pleasure boaters capsize and drown there with alarming frequency.

The first exit over the North River leads to Marshfield, another coastal town along the Irish Riviera, part bedroom community, part summer resort. From my early adolescence through mid-teen years our family summered at Marshfield instead of on the Cape because it was a quicker hop to Boston for my commuting father, at that time a high-ranking police officer. The city was simmering with racial tension then, and he had to be on constant alert, ready to respond at a moment's notice to potentially inflammatory incidents.

My memories of those summers exiled to Marshfield are ambivalent; we had a nice cottage with an ocean view, but for me the bottom line was that it wasn't Cape Cod. Congenitally Cape-centric, I thought Marshfield sorely lacked the other resort's charisma. You didn't have to cross great bridges to reach it, and I found it difficult to warm to a place where a wade into the sea induced instant paralysis from the cold. Having grown up splashing about in Buzzards Bay and Nantucket Sound—which are like bathtubs in summer—I found Marshfield's ocean waters so arctic as to be intolerable. Even Thoreau, with his hard-shelled reputation, found South Shore bathing tough to take. After attempting a swim at Cohasset, he commented, "It was one of the hottest days in the year, yet I found the water so icy cold I could swim but a stroke or two."

Halfway through Plymouth, right on schedule, the Boston forecast of "sunny all across the region today" was mocked as usual when the sun disappeared behind a glittery overcast. Of course, had the forecasters predicted rain for Boston, the converse would have applied. The weather patterns in Boston invariably flip-flop once you get to Plymouth, where Route 3 sends a fork left, leading to the local historic sites. In winter this is also the usual line of demarcation between snow to the north and rain to the south.

Plymouth is also where the landscape begins to assume a topography common to the imminent peninsula, distinguished by sandier soil and a proliferation of pitch pine and oak trees— "scrub" oak we always called them, "shrub" oak to Thoreau. When this highway first opened—it must have been in the late 1950s or early 1960s—the pines and oaks were little more than seedlings, and you could see forever across the barren reaches. But the forest has sprouted up quite a bit over the years and is not so scrubby (or shrubby) anymore. As a result, the vistas are more limited than they used to be. Of course, there's not much to see around these parts besides more of what Henry James unkindly called the region's "shabby woods."

Traffic was light for the start of a holiday weekend, and an hour or so out of Boston we entered the mainland part of Bourne, the first town on Cape Cod. When I was a youngster traveling to the Cape by our favorite route, the old Cranberry Highway (Routes 28 and 6), my parents would give prizes to us kids as we spotted landmarks that meant we were nearing the promised land: *"Ocean Spray! The White Rabbit Tea Room! The Railroad Bridge! Bourne Bridge!"* Now ahead was the Bourne Bridge's twin, and I had an urge to shout out *"Sagamore Bridge!"* (But would the bus driver reward me with a piece of saltwater taffy?)

The P&B strained its way to the top of the Sagamore, and in time-honored tradition I strained out of my seat to watch for big ships on the Cape Cod Canal below. Monica Dickens has called the Sagamore and Bourne those "soaring . . . bridges," and though I've been at this zenith hundreds of times, as always my heart soared at the fording, my gut tingled, and it took a physical effort to choke back a welling surge of gladness. The Cape's hold on me is visceral, and I was momentarily nearly overcome by waves of memory and desire.

Cape Cod's two great vaulting gateways, arched over the canal like silver rainbows, might have been designed by an architect with a poetic streak, for they are metaphors in steel—beginning here, at the confluence of low-lying coastal plain and expansive ocean, New England's own Big Sky country opens up. In the city I've often felt like a specimen trapped in a petri dish, with the buildings and even the sky pressing down on me like a lid screwed on too tight, but down here the lid pops off, and I am released into one of nature's premier broad expanses. Even though I was still in the bus, already I felt lighter, freer.

A Place Apart is the title of an excellent anthology of Cape-inspired writing. Crossing the bridge that day, I realized how apt that title is. The Cape *is* a place apart, literally—it is cut off from the rest of Massachusetts by the world's widest sea-level canal; thus it is as much an island as it is a peninsula. Technically, the canal is a man-made achievement (and an outstanding one at that), but it's only right to acknowledge that nature laid the groundwork. As the glaciers that formed Cape Cod retreated, dammed-up waters slicing through hilly Scusset left a deep gash across the narrow isthmus, in effect performing basic engineering work that paved the way for twentieth-century steamshovels. I'm often reminded of the canal's natural origins on blue-skied winter days following a snowfall, when the canal can be so blindingly, icy pure, like a great polar stream, that you'd almost think its waters gushed from glaciers still, springing perhaps from an ice floe that's hidden just beyond the bend at Herring Run, and melting away for eternity.

At the Sagamore's Cape end we passed one of the famous Christmas Tree Shops, and with skies looking less and less promising the store was being besieged by disappointed beachgoers. This outlet is the flagship store of a discount chain now retailing a wide range of consumer goods, but the concept has its roots in local gift/craft shops that years ago began to thrive on the Cape, selling winter's holiday wares to summer tourists. Seeking to get more bang for the buck out of what was back then a short season, shrewd Yankee merchants hit subliminal paydirt, and a visit to a "Christmas" shop for trinkets to be unwrapped and displayed on the year's longest nights became an indispensable part of the Cape Cod vacation experience.

I must have been four or five when I first encountered a Cape Christmas Shop (most likely on a washed-out beach day), and I thought I'd died and gone to heaven. What sort of magical place was this Cape Cod? Here you could have your cake *and* eat it too! At that instant, summer vacation on Cape Cod and Advent — those solstice soulmates whose celebrations marked the two high points of my childhood calendar — became inextricably linked in my impressionable mind, forever consigned to share space in that attic where fondest memories are stored. For me, Cape Cod and

Christmas would not be an illogical pairing in a shrink's free-association quiz.

We rode past Sandwich on Route 6, the main Cape highway. Gaps showed on wooded ridges where trees had been flattened, still visible reminders of Hurricane Bob of 1991, the Halloween northeaster (or "No-Name" storm of the same year), and other cataclysmic tempests that have roared through here in the past few years. At this moment a stiff breeze was animating the trees left standing, their massed clusters of leaves streaking white-bellied against the gray sky like schools of fish in mad flight from a predator.

Hardwood trees seen from Route 6 in Sandwich are natural successors to a forest that in the mid-nineteenth century girdled the Cape's middle as far as Orleans, a corridor that somehow escaped both the woodsman's efficient ax and Thoreau's attention. Thoreau wouldn't learn of the forest's existence until his 1857 journey (when a native mentioned it to him), and the clear-cut coastal areas he initially toured helped form his first impressions. While reading *Cape Cod*, I was astonished at the treeless place he described, for one of my first and most powerful impressions of the Cape was that it was *mostly* treed, covered by a forest Henry James might have thought shabby but looked to a city boy as extensive and grand as the Great North Woods.

Also central to my earliest memories of the Cape, so devoid of timber in the eighteenth and nineteenth centuries that natives depended on what drifted in from the sea, was its potpourri of woodsy aromas: the resinous bouquet of standing pitch pines (I thought the Cape even *smelled* like Christmas) as well as those felled to make way for the postwar construction boom; the scent of freshly sawed lumber stacked everywhere to build new cottages; the sharp varnish smell of every knotty pine cottage interior; and the burnt offerings of a thousand working fireplaces and woodstoves that, mingling with a raw ocean wind on chilled summer days, left the Cape smelling like one big smoked herring. Ah, to breathe deep and get a whiff of the Cape! To my young nostrils it was an olfactory factory.

The first third of the peninsula you encounter, which includes Sandwich, Bourne, and Falmouth, is known as the Upper Cape; the second section, from Barnstable to Harwich, is known as the Mid-Cape; and the outer extremities are called the Lower Cape, or down Cape. These designations tend to baffle visitors, as "Upper Cape" Sandwich lies well to the southwest of "Lower Cape" Provincetown; even some locals are thrown by the apparent paradox.

The explanation is fairly simple: the names stem from sailing days, and are based on the direction of the prevailing "sow'west" winds. To get from, say, Sandwich to Provincetown, you would sail with the wind—downwind—or "down." (This is also why we go "down" to Maine.) The return trip would be upwind, or "up" to Sandwich. Thoreau also used this terminology: in *Cape Cod* he mentions how a Pilgrim hunting party went "up" to Truro from Provincetown.

Our bus hit the last commuter lot, at Exit 6 in Barnstable. This was as far as the Mid-Cape Highway extended when I was young, the old oranged-roofed Howard Johnson's at the long-gone rotary now replaced by a new landmark, a Burger King flying a mammoth American flag, the largest display of the colors I'd ever seen. (Who says New Englanders have no appetite for excess? Texas, eat your heart out.)

Next stop was Hyannis, the Cape's hub. The outskirts of the town feature a few rustic motels on a large pond, calling to mind a lakeside resort, Lake George or perhaps Laconia. But from

Phinney's Lane on in, Route 132 is now totally malled, and as we crawled through bumper-to-bumper traffic toward the East End terminal, the only sights to see were sprawling shopping centers, home to super-supermarkets, auto dealerships, big national chain stores, and the Cape Cod Mall. Route 132, hosting the most intensive concentration of commerce on the entire Cape, has become every Cape Cod lover's worst nightmare, an apocalyptic vision, some say, of the rest of the peninsula's ultimate fate if its explosive growth isn't controlled.

That's a point well taken. Still, you could argue that not all the ramifications of Hyannis development are negative. By serving as the Cape's historic magnet for large-scale business, Hyannis has allowed other parts of the Cape to retain more of their charm (although it's true that versions of the Hyannis strip have now blossomed in the more populous towns). Locally, one unexpected and heartening backlash against highway mega-growth has been the renaissance of Main Street, Hyannis's old downtown district. Entrepreneurs have rehabbed formerly boarded-up stores, and mall-weary tourists have rediscovered the pleasures of strolling and browsing in funky little shops. Outdoor cafes have flourished, and watching the parade pass on a summer's eve from the vantage point of sidewalk cafes has become one of this big village's more agreeable attractions.

The bus arrived at the P&B terminal in a tired-looking East End block, just across from a miniature golf course where players could get a dose of Cape history while putting about. Each hole was decorated with an authentically rendered, scale-modeled local landmark, evocative of bygone days: a lighthouse and a windmill, naturally, along with a Quaker meetinghouse, a fisherman's shanty, and so on, eighteen symbols of Old Cape Cod altogether, which just about exhausts the theme. If the course's proprietors ever decide to expand, they might have to cheat a little into the twentieth century and add replicas of the pizza parlor, the package store, and the penny arcade.

Hyannis was the destination for most of the passengers, and the bus emptied quickly. Many of the departing were greeted at the terminal, and there was much kissing and hugging while luggage was loaded into waiting cars. I always feel a certain wistfulness viewing such scenes; in my mind all the visitors and their hosts are off to great homes by the ocean, where seabreezes luff crisp curtains in neat guest rooms, and cold cocktails are poured on the veranda when the boom of the yacht club cannon signals day's end.

We would be here only for a brief layover, and that was just fine with me—Hyannis did not play any part whatsoever in Thoreau's *Cape Cod*.

II. Old King's Highway

Across from the bus terminal, a big Amtrak diesel was parked on a siding at the old railroad station. During the layover, my thoughts wandered to the Cape Cod Railroad, whose story in many respects reflects Cape Cod's vicissitudes over the past century and a half, including its traditional propensity to get caught up in boom and bust economic cycles.

In October 1849, after the Boston-Provincetown boat was held up by the big storm that wrecked the *St. John,* Thoreau and Channing wended their way down the South Shore, eventually stopping at Bridgewater for the night. The next day they caught a train to Sandwich, at that time the railroad's terminus. Previously concerned that the coming of the railroad to Concord would alter his hometown's rural, self-reliant nature, Thoreau made no comment on its incursion on the Cape. As it turned out, the railroad would have a far greater impact on the Cape than it ever had on Concord.

Extending to Provincetown by 1873, Cape Cod Railroad (later, after a merger, the Old Colony) and its branches opened up the peninsula for a nascent tourist trade while providing local tradesmen a cheap and reliable means to tap into the far-flung, expanding American marketplace. (Among exports were eighteen carloads of Wellfleet oysters *daily*, according to one report—could that have been possible?) The very face of Cape Cod changed as the old towns found their place in this world topsy-turvy: towns on the Upper Cape—Bourne, Sandwich, Falmouth—difficult to reach before rail but now first stops on the lines from Boston and New York, grew in proportion to their new accessibility, while some towns down Cape became more isolated with the phasing out of bay-crossing steamers and began to stagnate.

For fifty years or more, trains were *the* way to get to Cape Cod, but the introduction of mass-produced automobiles in the 1920s and the opening of the canal auto bridges in the 1930s swiftly ended Cape Cod Railroad's hegemony. In time, lines were abandoned, and tracks fell into sorry disrepair. For decades the old infrastructure lay neglected, weed-choked, and all but forgotten.

Today, by submitting to the whims of the market and modern Cape demands, the once all-powerful railroad has made something of a modest comeback here. On a refurbished but truncated line, Dennis to the canal, freight cars carry off Cape Cod's greatest modern export—garbage—for incineration at a trash-to-energy plant in nearby Rochester, Massachusetts, thus obviating the further expansion of unsightly, polluting landfills. The remainder of the line, the old right-of-way from Dennis through the outer Cape, has been given over to a popular "rail trail" for pedestrians and cyclists.

A few years ago, in a burst of enthusiasm for public transportation, passenger rail from Boston was revived, but that was in the gung-ho 1980s, during the Massachusetts "Miracle," when there was public money for seemingly everything. Eventually the economy plummeted, the state's rail subsidy ended, and the line reverted to being a short-hop "scenic" railroad. Few miss the Boston passenger trains, which were poorly patronized — the average Cape Cod traveler's love affair with the car remains as ardent as the Californian's. (The only passenger train running in the early 1990s was a once-weekly Metroliner from Penn Station, since canceled by Amtrak.)

At the moment I was on a modern stagecoach, larger but otherwise not greatly dissimilar to the conveyance Thoreau and Channing took along the Old King's Highway (now Route 6A) to Orleans after leaving their train in Sandwich. When Thoreau boarded his stage (a mode of transportation soon made obsolete by the railroad), he was impressed both by its egalitarianism and by the "free and easy" nature of the passengers. He also mentioned that the women's faces seemed "pinched up" owing to poor dental work, while the menfolk appeared "pickled." Now my bus began to fill with a fresh crop of travelers, who also seemed free and easy — though none appeared either pinched or pickled.

Packed with passengers bound for the Lower Cape, the P&B coach left the terminal, heading down Willow Street to Yarmouth and the bay side of the Cape. Behind us were the commuter parking-lot stops of creeping suburbia; ahead, according to the timetable, the bus would pull in at Peterson's Market, the Post Office, the General Store, Town Hall, the Village Green—"Heck, I'll let you off wherever you want," announced the driver, "so long's you give me fair warning."

I never thought the big bus would maneuver the turn onto narrow Route 6A at the Yarmouth Christmas Tree Shop, but it did, and—forward into the past—instantly we entered Old Cape Cod, the idyllic Cape of popular song and picture postcard. Here now were the bed and breakfasts and rambling country inns, the barns turned "antiques" shops and second-hand bookstores, the classic old homes.

In addition to exuding genuine antique charm, homes along 6A, even those doing double duty as overpriced gift shops and modern art galleries, are uniformly lacking in ostentation and frilly adornment. This sense of decorous understatement is shared by the more recently built structures, for from Sandwich to Orleans the Old King's Highway is a protected historic district, where simplicity of style is no longer just a tradition, it's also a mandate.

The first settlement we passed was the picturesque village of Yarmouth Port, with Hallet's store and its old-fashioned soda fountain. The trees lining the road here are tall if not towering, affording 6A adequate shade and adding an "Old Home Week" touch to the small-town scene. In a bit of a departure from other sections of the highway, most houses in this village are set flush to the road, almost within spitting distance of passing traffic.

Thoreau painted a stark picture of desolation along the Old King's Highway, but the architectural styles of numerous residences lining 6A in Yarmouth Port—saltbox, traditional Cape, Georgian, Federalist, Greek and Gothic revival—indicate that most were built before 1849, and Yarmouth Port must have been a fairly thriving hamlet then, at least by Concord standards. Thoreau did not record specific impressions of this village — perhaps because of the pelting rain he did mention, a downpour that often obscured his stagecoach views.

The views from my window were unobscured, and I could see that with a few "modern" commercial complexes scattered about, and with an abundance of verdure that had not yet taken root in 1849, today's Yarmouth Port is not quite the same place Thoreau missed in the rain. But the fundamental look and feel of the Old King's Highway remain closer to the nineteenth century than to the twenty-first, and while Thoreau might require some acclimation time if he came to town today, certainly my late grandparents would be right at home on the present 6A, a road whose rural atmosphere has not changed greatly since they first tootled along here in their Model-T during the Harding administration.

After passing Dennis village and its famous summer theater, we drove by surprisingly large tracts of undeveloped Dennis land from Scargo Hill to Sesuit Harbor and beyond. While riding through "sublimely dreary" Dennis on the stage, Thoreau wondered where its "one hundred fifty masters of vessels" resided, and correctly surmised that "there must be many more houses along the south side of town." The south side is still the more thickly settled; ever since Cape Cod became a vacation and retirement destination, the bulk of visitors and homesteaders have been drawn to Nantucket Sound's seasonally tepid waters. That the bay side bears the uncluttered country look of Old Cape Cod rather than of an overrun seaside resort is due in no small part to a widely held preference of bathers for shores kissed by the warming Gulf Stream over those brushed by the Gulf of Maine's cool lips.

Passage through Dennis reminded Thoreau that this was the hometown of Captain John Sears, the first American to perfect a way of obtaining salt from seawater through evaporation. In the 1830s more than four hundred saltworks operated on the Cape, enterprises whose enormous appetites for firewood contributed to the decimation of local forests and subsequent soil erosion. But by 1849 this industry was in decline following the discovery of salt deposits out west, and Thoreau wrote that "from making salt, they turn to fishing more than ever." And now, with the fishing industry all but wiped out, what will native workers turn to? Sadly, Cape Cod's history is stained by a recurring depletion of its natural resources.

Through breaks in roadside shrubbery, I could see a salt marsh rolling in the direction of the bay, marked with small thickets of trees standing out on the broad plain, dry oases in the expanse of wetland. Momentarily Cape Cod Bay itself showed, wedged into a narrow slot between land and sky. Even this fleeting glimpse of salt water was powerfully evocative, and like John Cheever's midwestern tourist looking out at the Mediterranean, I wondered why the sea was something I remembered in my marrow. The bay was nearer than it appeared, only a mile or so away, but through Plexiglas it seemed as far off as a distant galaxy. The state of anticipation can be a delightful thing, but mine was building to a frustrating, almost unbearable level; suddenly wanting desperately to be on the beach, I squirmed in my seat with "Daddy-Are-We-There-Yet?" antsy-ness.

The bay view vanished as we entered Brewster, named after the Pilgrim William Brewster. ("Who has not heard of Elder Brewster? Who knows who he was?" asked Thoreau.) To Thoreau, prosperous Brewster seemed the most "modern-built town" on the Cape, whereas today it's the quintessentially quaint Cape Cod village. The old-fashioned, blue gingham–curtained general store, draped for summer in patriotic bunting, is one of the peninsula's most photographed objects and a local magazine cover favorite. The sea captains' homes that so impressed Thoreau are now B&Bs and inns.

In the old days, according to Brewster chronicler Reverend John Simpkins, the townspeople were a notoriously sober lot ("More than can be said of my townspeople," Thoreau grumbled), "not a proper idler or tavern-haunter in the place." Today's Brewster, however, strikes me as a more likely spot for a convivial drink than austere, abstemious, self-controlled contemporary Concord, where I imagine the drinking class is not readily welcome. One of the most wildly popular pouring establishments on the entire Cape nowadays is a place in Brewster called the Woodshed, a bar featuring top musical entertainment, which on any given night draws improper idlers and tavern haunters from Hyannis to Provincetown.

My immediate destination was Orleans, that pretty town at the crook of Cape Cod's arm. If America had remained part of Great Britain, Orleans is the kind of place (Chatham is another) to which retired officers of the colonial service would have come to live out their days after serving the crown, content to tend gardens and rosebushes by tidy, trellised cottages. But on this holiday weekend Orleans would set even an old imperialist's stiff upper lip to quivering, for the town—at least during the summer—has become the Hyannis of the Lower Cape, and the Saturday noon traffic was extremely heavy and slow-moving.

At last, the bus let us Orleans passengers off downtown. Thoreau started walking from nearby Higgins Tavern; this was close enough. The hike was about to be on.

KAROL B. WYCKOFF

2

Get Thee Behind Me

A storm in the fall or winter is the time to

visit [the Outer Cape]; a man may stand

there and put all America behind him.

CAPE COD

The Orleans bus stop is near the Land-Ho!, a popular bar-restaurant. The good old Ho! I ducked in, hoping to grab a little lunch before hitting the road. This is a most pleasant public house, sometimes boisterous, always good-natured. Like the modern Cape as a whole, it is a place where diversity is tolerated if not celebrated outright. At the Ho!, as elsewhere on the Cape, the denizens may not mingle much — fishermen types in their flannel shirts gravitate to the bar while tweedy retirees fill the tables — but by and large they coexist peacefully in an atmosphere of laissez-faire neighborliness.

I don't mean to suggest that Cape Cod is a utopia; rather, the new cosmopolitan Cape embodies many of society's stubborn polarities, including the ever-widening division between rich and poor. But the necessities of small-town living (and cash under the table) tend to bring people together across chasms of class, and in outer Cape towns such as Orleans the gentry and the yeomanry are not unaware of their mutual dependence. At the Land-Ho!, which serves as both clearinghouse for the disparate population's information and brokerage house for important transactions, you might on occasion overhear property owners informally hiring contractors and then perhaps cementing the deal with a drink.

The uneasy confederacy of natives and newcomers, young blue collar and retired white collar, has held together for the most part through some of the most turbulent years in Cape history. The one major fissure in the general *modus vivendi* that I know of came in the late 1980s, when some Cape residents were calling for a building moratorium, which would have put a whole lot of people out of work—things got pretty ugly for a while.

The Land-Ho! was mobbed, so I hit the road. It took me a few minutes to get my walking rhythm down—I had never worn a backpack before today. But soon I was cruising by the slowed auto traffic, passing motels, shops, a boatyard, lobster-in-the-rough shacks. At the junction of 6A and 28, Town Cove appeared on my right shoulder, and I was now bearing north, about to hook up with Route 6 again. Town Cove connects to Nauset Harbor, and like Thoreau I had to circumnavigate the Cove, the Harbor, and the Nauset Marsh beyond them to reach the uninterrupted stretch of strand that begins near Coast Guard Beach in Eastham, the next town.

At the Orleans-Eastham border stands one of the beacons of highway cuisine: a Dairy Queen. This DQ was serving take-out only and rather leisurely at that—"half fast" food, my father would have called it. I figured I'd be burning off thousands of calories over the next few days, so I waited patiently for two great, greasy double cheeseburgers and a giant mocha frappe, fat and cholesterol be damned. Abandon guilt and inhibition at the canal, all ye who cross it!

Just before a traffic rotary, a sign at a mini-mall called Jeremiah Square reminded me that I was crossing over the former location of Jeremiah's Gutter, a small waterway that Thoreau had forded. Now just a "folk memory" (to use Beston's term), the gutter cut across the Cape and connected Cape Cod Bay to Town Cove (an outlet to the ocean). It was used to evade a British man-o'-war stationed off Provincetown during the War of 1812.*

The rotary led me onto Route 6, where a sign reads, "Caution — Heavily Congested Next Thirty Miles." Actually, Route 6 is not too bad from here to Provincetown (only three miniature golf courses along the entire stretch), considering that it could easily have become another tacky horror like Route 28 in Hyannis-Yarmouth-Dennis. Although it sounds ominous, the "Congested" sign at Orleans Rotary serves mostly as fair traffic warning; the road that passes through the lightly populated outer Cape of the National Seashore *is* thickly settled in spots along its fringes and heavily traveled in season. From here on out Route 6 is sometimes four lanes, sometimes two, an undivided high-speed rural blacktop abutted by occasional unprepossessing commercial enclaves (convenience stores, trinket shops, motels, restaurants)

---

*A few years ago a Provincetown iconoclast named Jay Critchley proposed dredging out the old Gutter and restoring it to its former use. In his view, the Gutter could serve as a means of escape to the open Atlantic both for pilot whales who get trapped in the bay and for seaborne humans fleeing a meltdown of the nuclear plant in Plymouth, whose location near the canal would make any overland evacuation of the Cape nightmarish. Most people on the Cape laughed at Critchley and his dredging scheme, and I've a notion it wasn't proposed seriously anyway; more likely, he was making some sort of eco-political statement.

and intersected by innumerable pokey lanes running through pitch pine forest from ocean and bay beaches. Accidents involving turns onto or off Route 6 are regular occurrences, and there have been a number of fatal crashes over the years, some of them quite spectacular. Day in and day out, the Eastham-Provincetown segment of Route 6 is much more dangerous than the two-lane corridor of Route 6 from Exit 9 in Dennis to the Orleans Rotary sensationally nicknamed "Suicide Alley."

With Town Cove still on my right, I passed a small farmstand advertising native produce, and I remembered that Thoreau was amazed by reports of Eastham's bumper corn crops, for the outward appearance of the soil was poor. Like Thoreau, I had taken to reading local guidebooks and was myself surprised to learn from *The Little Yellow Cape Cod Guide* that "until the 1920s Eastham was known as the asparagus capital of the country." Eastham the Asparagus Capital. Of the U.S.A.

One of today's Cape agricultural marvels is not a farm product but the emerald green lawn. In 1972 Monica Dickens wrote about Cape Codders who complained that the grass wasn't as green as in England, despite all the moisture. But that problem has been solved by lawn care products (companies offering chemical lawn service were virtually unheard of here twenty years ago), often at the expense of the environment: chemical runoff has added to the degradation of many an inlet and marsh. Regrettably, the Cape has had to contend not only with its new multitudes but also with certain attitudes they bring along with them. Ostensibly here to enjoy a Cape Cod way of life, many of the recent arrivals can't wait to reproduce the suburbias they left behind, a graft which in many cases has taken poorly.

Thoreau entitled the Orleans-to-Eastham part of his journey

"The Plains of Nauset," and described a rolling expanse of sand holding little in the way of flora or fauna. The modern traveler finds the plains now mainly wooded, with trees and shrubs as well entrenched as on other parts of the Cape. At one roadside lot I saw probably more wood stacked into cords than had grown in all of Eastham in 1849. Nearby a woman was hanging out her wash, and impetuously I called to her, "What kind of wood is this?"

Looking more than a little perturbed about being interrupted in the middle of chores, she stalked over, and I steeled myself for a chewing out. I instantly recalled Thoreau's encounter in this same neighborhood with a woman "of a hardness and coarseness such as no man ever possesses," whose "jaws of iron" looked as if they could have bitten "a boardnail in two." But my Nauset matron was neither hard nor coarse and had neither bite nor bark; correctly sizing me up as a harmless sort of pest, her stern-faced reserve melted, and in no time we were engaged in friendly conversation.

She explained that the sawed logs (which were for sale) were what was left of two hundred locust trees that a succession of gargantuan gales had knocked down over recent years. Despite the damaging winds, her property was still thick with locusts, a handsome tree with criss-crossed bark that encases its trunk in a basket-weave pattern. The locust grows tall, and though the trunk is lean, it has a supple strength, like the legs of a long-distance runner. Some of the toppled trees were over a hundred years old, the woman told me, so they had to be tough to last that long in this hostile place. Indeed, Thoreau mentioned locusts as the single example of tree thriving in Eastham.

"They don't need much aging, and they burn sweetly," the woman said as she waved me back on my way. I noticed that the grass beneath the remaining locusts was green and lush, and remembered that locusts are nitrogen fixers, trees that create their own fertilizer from nitrogen taken in from the atmosphere. Perhaps Cape Codders who desire beautiful lawns could simply plant locusts and they'd be able to achieve the country club look naturally. The grass is always greener over the septic tank, and under the locust tree.

Thoreau's trek across the sandy plains of Nauset took so long and was so unrelenting—it seemed to take hours—that he burrowed into a history of Eastham to pass the time, reading as he walked. Eastham's history was essentially the history of the church in town, "that being the only story they have to tell," or more accurately, the only story then deemed worthy of being set in type. The ecclesiastical history, along with the presence nearby of a revivalist campground called Millennium Grove, prompted Thoreau to fire off a number of well-aimed, very funny barbs at some of his favorite targets: the established church, its evangelical splinters, and the clergy.

Whom do you suppose Thoreau might care to knock if he were traveling on the Cape today? Devilish developers? Some of the bad guys' clients? The humorist Dennis Miller once remarked, "A developer is someone who wants to build a house in the woods; an environmentalist is someone who already has a house in the woods." He seems to have hit the bull's-eye on the Cape, where new residents appear to get the green religion the moment their names are affixed to a Cape Cod deed. They want the Cape always to stay the way it was when they first moved here (even if only fifteen minutes ago) and damn anyone who would be presumptuous enough to follow their example: "Cape's getting too damn crowded." Although the Cape has gained over 50,000 permanent, year-round residents during the past two decades, I've yet to meet any who consider themselves at all culpable for problems associated with growth. No, the fellow who came over the bridge after them is the problem.

It was time to banish such thoughts, for the overdeveloped Cape of treated lawns and corner video stores was not to be found here in Eastham. Soon I was past the old windmill Thoreau wrote about, the Town Hall, which postdates him, and the brand new police station. Up ahead I could see the Salt Pond, and its visitors' center, the formal entrance to Cape Cod National Seashore.

At this point the Cape Cod Rail Trail, the bike path built on the old railroad right-of-way, funnels bikers out to the Seashore entrance, with Coast Guard Beach less than a mile away. I started for the beach on the bike path extension, but it was too crowded with both bikes and pedestrians, so I returned to the road. There was such a steady procession of traffic, cars and bikes alike, that to protect life and limb I had to hug the shoulder of the road, keeping watch over my own shoulder. Cars whizzing by bothered me only half as much as the cyclists. The whirring of spokes was deceptive, for it had the pleasant sound of a breeze whispering through the pines, but I soon came to associate it with an impending bark: "On your *left.*" Yes, I know you're not burning fossil fuels, now be quiet. Many of the bikers were couples my age, with kids in tow, each crimson-faced, helmeted youngster puffing and straining to keep up with the adults.

On the walk to Coast Guard Beach, evergreens predominated—spruce, pine, hemlock, cedar—in some cases standing in neat arrangement, looking almost ornamental, as if they had a landscaper to tend them. I took one quick diversion into the woods to view Doane Rock, a massive stone half-buried in the earth, carried by glaciers and deposited here when the great ice sheets began to melt and retreat northward. Some say Doane

Rock came from around Dedham, near where I live southwest of Boston; others say it's from as far north as New Hampshire—in any case, from a good distance. I salute thee, fellow traveler, but unlike you I must be going!

There was no gradual shift from forest to moor and dune country; one moment I was standing next to good-sized pines, the next I walked into a country of low brush. Suddenly, like a great actor who commands the stage the instant he emerges from the wings, not just appearing but making an *appearance,* there was the Atlantic, nature's Barrymore, magnetic, impressive, mesmerizing. The scene filled me with a sense of déjà vu, and for a moment I could almost believe in reincarnation—if I've ever lived before, sure it was as a seafaring man.

Next a broad seashore panorama hove into full view, low, rolling, brushy backdune giving way to sandy foredune, and just beyond, the beach. To the right on a high bluff sits the old Coast Guard station, built in the 1930s; to gain easy access to the beach proper, I had to follow the road that rises up to the station.

Along my path a forlorn pitch pine was growing at a sharp angle inland, looking as if it were trying to sneak away from the beach environs before it was noticed going AWOL. Destructive salt-laden winds had pruned the pine into the shape of a wild, ragged, fantastic musical note (sea sharp?), and indeed the pine seemed to be whistling out a plaintive warning, which could well have been: *You have reached the edge of North America, east and ahead. Proceed at your own peril.* Having come this far, I decided I would take my chances.

The bluff offers a superb view south to Nauset Marsh, where today at low tide sinuous channels made innumerable islands out of exposed tidal flats. Somewhere out there along the marsh's protective barrier beach, Henry Beston built his legendary cottage, the "Outermost House," where he lived alone for a year and which was finally claimed by the Blizzard of 1978. Beston, an outstanding writer and observer, is very important in the Cape Cod canon. His 1928 book gives us a sense of what the Cape was like in the epoch between Thoreau's time and our own, those late halcyon years when Old Cape Cod was on the brink of its modern incarnation.

The Coast Guard station, whose predecessor Beston often visited during the year he lived on the beach, is now used as a center for environmental studies. One of the outdoor interpretative exhibits nearby displayed a picture of the old Coast Guard Beach parking lot, an asphalt monstrosity plunked down between marsh and beach on top of fragile dunes in the direction of the Outermost House. Like Beston's cottage, the parking lot was a victim of the Blizzard of '78. The fading sepia-toned photo, circa 1960, showing Ramblers, Chevys, and Ford woodies parked where now humans are barred from tern and plover nesting areas, looked to me almost make-believe, like movie stills from that era's science fiction films, needing only Godzilla breaking through waters offshore to complete the unreal scenario.

That egregious reminder of days when it was common practice to "pave Paradise" got me to musing about the environment again. The basic tenets of the environmentalists' faith are sound and admirable, and I'll be the first to acknowledge that green movements and increased ecological awareness have been lifesavers around the globe and certainly on the Cape. It's just a pity that so many embrace the creed for dubious motives, or pay it mere lip service.

From the bluff's peak I scanned the wide expanse of gray-green ocean to its far edge, "the rim of the world" in Beston's words, the vantage point providing clear evidence of the earth's curvature. (Sometimes I wonder how any civilization set on the slightest elevation overlooking the sea could ever have thought the earth was flat.) Before descending, I paused for a final briefing with Beston, at a placard bearing his admonishment to the beach visitor: *"Listen to the surf, really lend it your ears, and you will hear in it a world of sounds."* I will, I promised, I will.

A wide, graded boardwalk led me to the beach. Halfway down I took off sneakers and socks, and when my feet hit the warm sand I believed that no shipwrecked mariner reaching this shore from the *other* direction could have felt much better than I did at that moment. I almost gave the beach a kiss of gratitude, but there were people around, though not all that many, as the day had remained overcast.

A young woman outfitted in a wet suit approached from behind, and I stepped aside to let her go by. Just as she passed the little surfer stubbed a toe on a small rock, did an awkward little shuffle, and finally lurched into me, the sharp point of her board dinging me in the breastbone. *Ooofff!*

"Oh, I am *so* sorry!" she cried, her apology punctuated with a barely suppressed laugh.

"Quite all right," I managed to gasp when my wind returned. One minute on the Great Beach and already I'd learned several new applications for the expression "breathtaking."

After watching her descend into the sea, I shifted my thoughts to Thoreau. *New Yorker* writer Adam Gopnik, who first cracked open his *Cape Cod* while lounging on Nauset Beach during vacation, came to regard Thoreau almost as a companion, an "invented" Thoreau to whom he felt obliged to explain the beach's transmogrifications since 1849. I also felt a responsibility to clarify the modern Cape scene when necessary for the unseen *fidus Achates* beside me. But how to address him?

Using just the surname *Thoreau* sounded cold, distant, and academic. On the other hand, calling him Henry, or Henry David, seemed a mite *too* familiar. H.D.T., I'm afraid, sounded too much like a pesticide—but what about H.T.? Yes, I liked that; it was friendly yet not without a gentlemanly ring, somewhat in the style of the South, and God knows we New Englanders could stand some Southern manners. For the rest of the trip, then, H.T. it would be.

With that settled, I would have directed H.T.'s attention to the surfers offshore waiting patiently for something to ride, and to the kids playing volleyball on the upper beach. In these two instances explanations would not be so difficult. H.T. agreed that the "duck does not take to the water with surer instincts" than the Cape Cod boy (and now add the Cape Cod girl), and what are our young surfers but the most resourceful and inventive ducks, taking to water in the accustomed Cape Cod manner? And as for volleyball, it's just a simple game using a net and round ball— there's no way such sport would be unintelligible to a Harvard man, particularly one who wrote in his journal about witnessing the early beginnings of a game known as "base-ball."

Neither would I have had to spend much time with H.T. expounding on the three-day weekend, since Thoreau the gadabout practically invented the modern American concept of leisure time. Looking far ahead, though, I thought Provincetown might take some explaining, as would the situation spreading out right at my feet—for a hundred yards ahead the sand was littered with dozens upon dozens of what locals sardonically call "beach whistles"—plastic tampon applicators.

(I later asked a Park Service official where the beach whistles had come from, since there are no open sewers or storm drains along the outer beach, and I knew they couldn't just have been left there; there were simply too many. "Who can say?" he shrugged, telling me it would be impossible to determine where or when the tampon tubes had escaped from the waste stream and entered the ocean stream. It was not inconceivable, he said, that the plastic had floated for years with the currents, traveling hundreds of miles before beaching on the National Seashore like so much driftwood.)

The beach crowd was smaller than I'd expected. Though I was warmed after hiking from Orleans, there was an end-of-season bite to the air, and even the volleyballers were wearing sweat-shirts. Far offshore, a large stationary mass of dark furrowed cloud floated serenely on the horizon like an inflated rubber raft. The balance of the sky was covered by clusters of elongated fluff the color and shape of Wellfleet oysters, their jagged edges lus-trous, radiating promise that the sun pearl might yet be revealed. But although the cloud ceiling was high and a quick sniff offered no hint of impending rain, I sensed that these oysters would not be shucked any time soon.

In one of my guidebooks I read that a sunny day at the beach holds the essence of the Cape Cod experience. While I would never wish away a pleasant summer's day, in my view today's conditions epitomized the classic Cape Cod afternoon, moody and uncertain, as in a Winslow Homer painting where the oceanic sky alternately glimmers and glowers, and you're never quite sure whether the storm Homer was depicting was gathering or blow-ing out to sea. On days like this the sky's intentions often remain ambiguous, leaving open for endless debate the tourist's agoniz-ing dilemma: "Should we chance it and go to the beach, or does it make more sense to head for the Christmas Tree Shop?"

The ocean was fairly calm, light breezes giving its surface a slightly nubbed texture so that it resembled a large bolt of her-ringbone tweed. It's said that incoming waves build up and "trip" over the shallows as they move shoreward, but today the waves were merely stumbling in. Still, this is open ocean beach and the surf, though light by Coast Guard Beach standards, was yet strong enough to topple any toddler who might play at ocean's edge.

Normal tides on the Cape's outer beach are relatively narrow in range, having a differential of only six to eight feet (astronomi-cal and storm-driven tides are another matter altogether). The tide was "out," the high-water line clearly marked by a row of very fine reddish brown seaweed, set down by the ebbing surf in a perfect double-helix pattern. Just offshore were small clumps of the same growth, like the particles on the beach having the consistency of cooked spinach put through a food processor.

Rising up from the plains of Nauset, the great cliff was an ar-resting sight, and I made straight for it. As I craned my neck to look up the mocha-colored heights, which were stubbly with shrubbery and pocked with small rocks and boulders, instantly I recognized that I wasn't in Patti Page's Cape Cod anymore, though I knew I was sure to fall in love with *this* Cape Cod just the same.

Geology was an infant science when H.T. walked the Cape, and thus he was able to dwell on the cliff's origins as "diluvian" and leave it at that. I would like to have left it at that; science is my bête noire and the prehistoric holds little interest for me. Nevertheless, I had boned up on Cape geology by reading two popular general texts, Robert Oldale's *Cape Cod and the Islands—The Geologic Story*, and Arthur Strahler's *A Geologist's View of Cape Cod*. Reading laboriously but doggedly, like a liberal arts student with one science requirement left standing between him and the degree, I picked up some rudimentary knowledge of the Cape's beginnings. Of course, in the end I was glad I did.

Essentially, the present Cape comprises materials deposited on top of an ancient coastal plain by the southerly advance of great glaciers thousands of years ago. To put it in the most simplistic terms, the glaciers scraped up and pushed everything before them like a child scooping out and moving beach sand with his or her hands. The advancing colossi of ice dug out deep depressions in the earth's surface, disgorging the dredged matter at or beyond the glacial margins; when the glaciers retreated and melted with subsequent global warming, the depressions filled with rising seawater to become bays and sounds, while the piled-up dredged scrapings formed Cape Cod, Martha's Vineyard, Nantucket, and Long Island. This activity ended ten thousand years ago; in geologic terms the Cape we know today is a youngster.

The cliff is not a giant sand dune. In fact, it's called a marine "scarp." The scarp is made up of glacial deposits, which include various soils, not just sand but clay, gravel, and other types of earth, the amalgam known as glacial till.

The term *scarp* is common to both geology and military science, and it invites comparisons: H.T. wrote that the bank resembled "the escarped rampart of a stupendous fortress," a description Beston also used. I will continue to use the term *cliff* to describe the marine scarp, even though Strahler says that *cliff* is technically inaccurate in that it suggests a vertical wall. Although it seems steeper, the scarp's angle of repose is generally around 30 degrees, since the "incohesive" deposits are constantly collapsing down the slope's face. Only the very top of the scarp is near to sheer.

Erosion is the prime fact of life here—three feet lost per

year—and Cotton Mather's prophecy that someday "codfish will swim on the highest hills of the Cape" will be realized in time, if any codfish remain to swim. Geologists estimate that Cape Cod will go the way of Atlantis in about another six thousand years. Its impermanence is yet another of its fascinating features—the Cape is wasting away, destined someday to become but a folk memory, no less than Jeremiah's Gutter. (Fortunately for the purposes of the present project, I did not have to concern myself with the Cape's ultimate fate much beyond this obligatory mention of it.)

Ahead of the cliff was Nauset Light, which since my visit has had to be moved back from its precarious position on the bluff's eroding margin.* On the day of my walk the lighthouse's uppermost reaches were wreathed in vapor, the piercing red/white/red/white strobe comforting while at the same time serving to warn me that it was growing later on a late summer afternoon, with quite a bit of ground yet to cover.

Strolling by Nauset Light, I looked up to see a wedding ceremony taking place on an adjacent lot. Perched together at the cliff's edge like figurines on a wedding cake, the bride and groom were dazzlingly attractive, their hair perfect in spite of a persistent breeze. The minister, a rotund, florid-featured man wearing an old-fashioned long bib collar, could easily have passed for one of the Cape Cod preachers H.T. took delight in tweaking, those hell-and-brimfire men of the cloth whose leather-lunged sermonizing Thoreau fancied could drown out the roar of the sea.

Five minutes beyond Nauset Light, the beach was empty. Even

---

*In a striking coincidence underscoring the relentless Atlantic's onslaught, both Nauset Light and Truro's Highland Light, their original foundations laid 126 years apart (in 1923 and 1797, respectively), had to be moved out of harm's way within months of each other in 1996.

though a good chunk of America's population is within a day's drive of the Cape and over 5 million visitors come to the National Seashore each year, not a single soul was in sight. I was walking on a shore as desolate as the one Thoreau encountered when he set out for Provincetown on a rainy Thursday in October 1849.

For the time being anyway, I'd really put America behind me.

Sand Fences

KAROL B. WYCKOFF

3

The Beach

It was not as on the map, or seen from the

stage-coach; but there I found it all out of

doors, huge and real, Cape Cod!

CAPE COD

I. Eastham

I decided to stay barefoot. The sand—with a texture between coarse and fine, somewhat like 100-grit sandpaper—was heavy and deep, with no spring to it at all, and I sank on every footfall. It was tough going, like slogging through dry quicksand. Summer's gentler conditions lead to an accretion of sand on the outer beach, deposits that winter storms withdraw (with interest) to build up the spits north of here, in Truro and Provincetown, and south from Nauset all the way to Monomoy Island, a barrier beach formation that dangles like an unraveling thread from the Cape's elbow at Chatham.

A two-foot-high ridge in the middle of the sand divided the beach into two distinct parts; geologists call the upper part the winter berm and lower part the summer berm. Forming the base of the upper beach, the ridge was neat and level, as if made by a bulldozer, and it stretched on and on, a perfect scale model of the parallel cliff.

The beach at this point was fairly broad, at seventy yards perhaps twice as wide as the bank was tall. Many observers have made note of the Eastham beach's gentle curve westward, but at the moment the shore appeared to be laid out all in a straight line, like an arrow pointing down Maine.

I moved back and forth on the beach to get different perspectives, and went over to the scarp once more for further study. In H.T.'s day, and even as late as Beston's time, the cliff top was bare, with a sand belt stretching back dozens of yards. Now, with plants and trees creeping seaward and the headland eroding inland, the crown is heavily vegetated in spots. In many places plant life crests over the top, and I spotted one small pine jutting out from the bank almost horizontally, aimed at the sea like a loaded harpoon.

With ravine-like crevices carved out here and there, and brush and roots exposed on its flat, mesa-like top, the earth-toned cliff summoned up an image of the American West, a mind picture the ocean's roar did not easily dispel. Even the desiccated plant life looked vaguely western, and indeed the wormwood plants growing at the base of the cliff are related to the sagebrush. I concluded that references to the West are not totally out of place here. The elements that make up the earth and the forces shaping them are relatively few, and resemblances are to be expected; in some superficial aspects, the banked outer beach of Cape Cod is not that far removed from the Arizona high desert.

There are no buildings on the cliff, of course, and few near it, although such is the steepness of angle that a city could be constructed just beyond the rim and it would still be invisible from the beach. There were no dwellings on or near the beach when Thoreau passed by, either, with the exception of the Humane, or "charity," houses.

Humane houses were sponsored and built by the Humane Society in the days before a more sophisticated lifesaving system was established along the coast. Small beach huts, they were designed to provide shelter for shipwrecked sailors until rescue parties could reach them or until conditions abated and they could find their own way off the beach. Openings in the cliff are few and far between, coming only at small breaks called hollows, and hunting for a hollow at the height of a storm would be like groping along a wall for a secret panel in the dark, a search against odds that could prove fatal to weakened, disoriented castaways.

H.T., fascinated by the Humane houses, returned to the topic over and over in *Cape Cod*. Examining one hut with Channing, he found it on the whole ill suited to serve its intended function, missing matches and straw, among other items. These gross inadequacies earned Thoreau's undying disdain: "And there we thought, how cold is charity! how inhumane humanity! This, then, is what charity hides!"

The lack of convenient passage to and from the beach would appear also to discourage the kind of casual beach stroller you find along virtually every other stretch of Cape Cod shoreline. Although I welcomed the solitude, the total absence of human presence north of Nauset Light puzzled me. It was still summer, after all, and while I wasn't expecting it to look like Coney Island, where were the few, the hearty, the adventurous? Where were those lovelorn legions who profess in newspaper personal ads to enjoy long walks on deserted beaches?

Even H.T. had bumped into a couple of "wreckers," men who picked over the beach looking for driftwood and cargoes off unfortunate ships. But none of the wreckers' modern counterparts, those scavengers who haunt beaches with metal detectors, were out hunting for treasure on this strand today—metal detectors are banned from the National Seashore.

Back at surf's edge I had an unexpected close encounter, of the avian kind—a tern cruising south suddenly found me directly in its flight path. On a bearing for my head at full throttle, the startled bird made a rapid shift worthy of a Top Gun and veered away at the last instant. Go near a tern's nest in spring, and a flock of them will dive-bomb you until you move away, but this was not nesting season, and I detected no aggressive intent on the tern's part. Rather, its whole attitude seemed to ask, "What the heck is one of *you* doing out here?"

The tern went back on course and continued south, where it would find more of my kind at Nauset Light and Coast Guard beaches. Meanwhile, I had gathered up a small entourage of shore birds around me, mostly herring gulls and a band of sanderlings. The little sanderlings preferred to be in the vanguard, fanning out in front like a reconnaissance unit. They had no real interest in me as long as I didn't venture too close; their preoccupation was with picking up morsels the waves swept ashore.

I was amused by their jerky Charlie Chaplinesque gait and impressed with their agility and unerring ability to dodge the incoming surf. They had their game of surf tag timed to a nanosecond. Down into the breach they would go, dashdashdashdash, then eateateateat, then dashdashdashdash back to shore one rapid step ahead of the incoming, then back again at the instant of the turning. I began to mimic them, for the skill would come in handy if ever I put my sneakers back on, and soon became fairly proficient—at least at the dash and dodge. I didn't attempt the gustatory portion of the exercise.

Delightful as the sanderlings' company was, I found myself scanning the skies in search of great flights of birds. The Cape is a key flyway for all sorts of migrators, and I had anticipated that the skies would be darkened by flocks heading for their winter grounds. A few years ago in late July or early August, a TV cameraman and I went to isolated Monomoy Island, a National Wildlife Refuge that serves as a kind of flyway comfort stop, to do a story on migrating birds. We were disappointed to find Monomoy deserted save for a few gulls. "Come back at the end of August, or in September, and you'll see all the birds you'd ever want to," the ranger had told us. And yet here it was September, and the skies over Eastham were as empty of birds as the beaches were of people. Possibly I was a week early for the great migration, or perhaps a week late. I thought of Thoreau's self-evaluation: "Methinks my seasons revolve more slowly than those of nature; I am differently timed." Differently timed—that's the story of my life.

A few years ago I witnessed the spring homecoming of the alewives (known locally as herrings) up Brewster's Stony Brook from the sea, headed to spawn in Mill Pond. It was like an old-timer's tall tale come to life: you really could almost walk across the stream on fishes' backs, so thickly did they fill the narrow waterway. A naturalist watching the scene with me commented that the alewives' impressive numbers indicated that "something was right with the earth." Today, I prayed that the absence of great flocks over the outer Cape wasn't a signal that something was *wrong* with the earth. I hoped the birds were *somewhere*—perhaps they flew mainly at night, or over Cape Cod Bay, or farther out over the ocean.

I continued to marvel at the sheer length of the glacial cliff. The top remained level for the most part, but occasional irregularities in contour and elevation lent an impression that the cliff was *undulating,* rollercoasting over the landscape toward infinity in the manner of the Great Wall of China. An illusion that the cliff was endless was heightened by an almost phantasmagoric clot of fog concealing its farther reaches, described by Beston as "that seemingly fixed rounding of vapor towards which one walks but at which one never arrives." The effect of the distant shroud bordered on the hypnotic, and dreamily I kept moving toward it.

A wave ran up the shore and grabbed me around the ankles, as if the ocean were seeking to draw my attention back from its earthen rival. I snapped to it. *"Listen to the surf,"* I reminded myself, *"really lend it your ears."*

It takes some time to sort out and discern all the various surf sounds; like any music, at first it's mostly generic cacophony to the uninitiated. Although the offshore remained fairly calm, the surf had by now worked itself up into a fine froth, and as the spent waves backwashed into the sea they stirred a narrow band of cobblestones at the waterline. The resulting sound was just like applause—the cobbles seemed to be applauding the surf's energetic performance, briskly but appreciatively, the way an opera crowd might hail a well-sung aria by an indisposed diva's understudy. Next a medium-sized wave ran shoreward and flipped over quickly, making a riffling sound like a deck of cards being shuffled. Again the ebb agitated the rocks, which this time clicked together in a way that reminded me of a game of craps.

I'm not a gambling man—why did I have it on the brain? H.T. called the beach "the *true* Atlantic House," Thoreauvian wordplay that alluded to a famous Provincetown establishment, still standing today. Mightn't we also say that the Great Beach is "the true Atlantic *City*"? Certainly, both pleasure and risk reside here along the quartz boardwalk, where there's never a cover, and never a minimum.

Boom! Now there was a wave! It had been building, building, building, ready to edge over into a graceful curl when suddenly the bottom fell out and the wave simply imploded, collapsing in on top of itself, like a structure demolished by dynamite. *Boom!* I'd read the dictionary definition of the word "plangent" but never really *heard* plangent until I came to the beach. I also detected a note of violence in the percussion, which initially sounded like one car slamming into another broadside without braking. But it was more complex than that—the heavy waves produced a deeply elemental sound, one of the thunderous recurring notes of the beach's primal composition that even today can stir up what Beston called an "ancient terror" in the heart. Then, one, two, three sharp reports from the next series of waves.

The incoming waves deserved some visual appreciation as well. A large swell approached, but instead of breaking forward and landing in one big "wahoomp," it started cresting and crashing sideways down the shoreline, falling over like dominoes, *wahoomp wahoomp wahoomp wahoomp wahoomp wahoomp,* as neatly synchronized as the Rockettes' high-kick routine. Spectacular! Yes, the "true" Atlantic City!

The wind was blowing from shore and had freshened considerably, shearing the tops from breakers and tossing them seaward, so that the spume resembled the "white manes" of Neptune's horses, to use H.T.'s words. James Joyce used almost identical phrasing in *Ulysses;* in fact, "flying manes" has been a standard description for windswept wavetops since Homer, being one of those similes that nails an image so perfectly it can't be outdone.

I could never top Homer, Joyce, and Thoreau, but I could take their classical imagery a step further—not only could I see the sea god's steeds charging, I could *hear* them as well, their clattering hooves resounding in the back-and-forth wash of surf over cobbles. Thanks to Beston's sage directives, I was learning to appreciate Thoreau's Cape Cod as a multimedia experience.

I continued walking, in a while noticing that my surroundings had remained virtually unchanged for untold minutes. The combers kept rolling in, sanderlings trailblazed, big-chested gulls maintained positions around me like a Praetorian guard, the sea cliff disappeared northerly behind mist, and it was all as in a tableau; despite constant motion around me, everything seemed frozen in place. It was a feeling not unlike being on a treadmill, and except for an utter trust in physical sensation, faith that my arms and legs were indeed propelling me forward, I would have sworn I was standing still. At this moment one of my favorite poems by Robert Frost, "Devotion," came to mind:

> The heart can think of no devotion
> Greater than being shore to the ocean—
> Holding the curve of one position,
> Counting an endless repetition.

Counting an endless repetition. Always walking, never arriving. The sensation became rather unnerving as time passed, but then the mist evaporated in a flash. I could see the cliff's end for the first time all day, and it was in descent. There was activity, and I approached it almost nervously—what had the mist been hiding?

It was Marconi Beach. I was in Wellfleet.

II. Wellfleet

Marconi Beach is named for Guglielmo Marconi, who sent the first transatlantic wireless message from here at the turn of the century. (The wireless station, long gone, also picked up the *Titanic*'s distress call in 1912.) Today it hosts a National Seashore rest area, reached by climbing a long, steep set of wooden stairs. As I started up to get a drink, the way was blocked by a couple of lounging Japanese teens. When their father spotted this he barked furiously, and they scrambled out of the way so quickly they're probably still picking splinters out of their bottoms. Two men passed me on the way down, headed for a little surf fishing. Their light tackle was more appropriate for Walden Pond than for the Great Beach, and I doubted they'd last more than a few casts.

At the top of the bank I had my drink at a fountain by the public restroom, a wooden structure well bleached by the elements. The area also offered a fine profile of flora that inhabit terrain back of the open beach. Near the bank's brim, sprigs of beach grass had been planted like hair plugs on a bald man's head, while farther back grew bayberry bushes, with their frosted blue fruits; low-lying bearberry, showing off plump red orbs called horse cranberries; and tufted rounds of dull green beach heather.

Beach heather (*Hudsonia tomentosa*) is also known as "poverty grass," a name dating back to the days of barren Cape Cod, when little else flourished. Thoreau disliked the pejorative cognomen and thought poverty grass worthy enough to adorn Barnstable County's coat of arms ("I should be proud of it"). Even when not in flower, poverty grass is oddly attractive, though my botanical nominee for the county coat of arms would have to be pitch pine, the poverty tree.

Scoping out the *beau rivage* from the heights proved a radical departure from sea-level observation, where there were other things to attract attention, and from Marconi Beach the panorama confirmed H.T.'s statement that "the Ocean was the grand fact there, which made us forget both bayberries and men." From shore, he wrote, "even the sedentary man here enjoys a breadth of view which is almost equivalent to motion," what we today might call a kind of virtual reality. That might explain why so many people are content to stay in their cars at beach parking lots and just stare at the ocean: they're moving over sand and sea vicariously.

Equivalent motion can take you only so far; I would need my sea legs to get to Wellfleet center, which more and more looked to be where I'd be putting up for the night. On the way back to the beach I passed the Japanese family on the steps, staring intently out to sea, as if they were trying to memorize the ocean's features. Incredibly, the two fishermen had disappeared from sight, on a beach where there's nowhere to hide. Perhaps they had lucked out and hooked some very large fish, and were presently offshore being taken on impromptu Nantucket sleigh rides.*

Between Marconi Beach and the small pavilion commemorating Marconi's achievement, the imposing cliff is scaled down, for here the Wellfleet plain becomes a salient thrusting right into the beach to form one of the scarp's rare large indentations. On this summer day the cascading slope was covered by a velvety carpet of jade beach grass, thick and lush as a well-watered Chia pet, which grew down to and over the outer edge of the winter berm. Common to beach fringes almost everywhere, the grassy mead-

---

*Nantucket sleigh ride is the term used to describe the wild ride across the waves given a pursuing whaleboat by a harpooned whale in flight.

owland here looked incongruous, even exotic, sprouting up in this gap between the sea cliff's severe walls.

The kinder, gentler topography lasted for about a quarter of a mile before the fortress rose again, at which point the beach sharply narrowed. Stretching across the path in front of me, the entire length from bank to ocean's edge, was a huge throng of gulls. Until now I'd encountered only small knots of the birds, but this appeared to be a whole colony, and they made me stop dead in my tracks. My first thought was of the teenage gangs in *The Blackboard Jungle*, which I'd seen recently. I was afraid that if I waded through the gang I might provoke them; on the other hand, if I skirted around them through the swash would they take me for a chicken, and be emboldened to harass me? Suddenly the whole flock took flight, some alighting offshore, the rest scattering down the beach. The gulls had blinked first, so to speak, and I proceeded undisturbed.

Herring gulls weren't always so numerous or ubiquitous on the Cape as they are today. When Thoreau passed through they were still migratory visitors from Maine and had yet to begin breeding locally. Back then the birds were hunted mercilessly, lured in large numbers to blinds on the beach and snatched by hand or shot; H.T. believed (erroneously, says Paul Theroux) that this practice spawned the term "to be gulled," meaning to be taken in by trickery. Gull feathers were fashionable adornments on women's hats in the nineteenth century, and like a number of other species gulls were almost driven to extinction for the millinery trade.

Hunting gulls has been outlawed since early in this century; today people must be content with just cursing them. Their only contribution to the contemporary millinery trade is as a subject of ridicule on baseball hats: seemingly every Cape tourist trap stocks headgear emblazoned with the words "Damn Seagulls!" accompanied by an appliqué of fake guano. (But when the U.S. Fish and Wildlife Service recently began poisoning and shooting gulls on Monomoy Island—purportedly to give terns and plovers a chance to nest in peace—Cape Codders went ballistic and called for a halt to the slaughter.)

I must admit that at the start of my walk I harbored some feelings of distaste for herring gulls, which struck me as being to the beach what pigeons are to city parks. While on the beach I did not see a single gull diving for a fish—in fact, at any time at least half were content to turn their backs on the sea and stare pointlessly at the cliff. And those eyes: to me they were a perfect illustration of the saying "the lights are on but nobody's home."

Yet the gulls' eyes belie a wily knack to make the best out of what's dealt them. Standing on a bridge over the River Liffey in *Ulysses*, Leopold Bloom observes that the gulls below him could tell whether he was tossing down a morsel of cake or a crumpled piece of paper almost before the objects left his hand. "Not such damn fools," he concedes.

No, they're not. Terns and plovers struggle but gulls thrive, getting fat through no discernible effort; some, the burly black-backed especially, attain the size of small eagles. Humans, of course, have been their most gullible providers; even on offshore Monomoy I've seen chicken bones and other human culinary detritus in empty gulls' nests, no doubt the pickings of Cape dumps and dumpsters. With most trash being shipped off-Cape and landfills being capped, would the gulls learn to fend for themselves once more? The prospect was chilling, and that scenario made me think of Hitchcock's movie *The Birds*. Once, at an outdoor restaurant on Hyannis Harbor, I saw a huge gull not only snatch a french fry out of a little girl's hand but also give her a nasty bite in the process. When all the garbage is gone, I wondered, would millions of starving gulls unleash a reign of terror on alfresco Cape Cod?

Moving along, I met up with another type of bird that does quite well on the outer Cape, the bank swallow. Though not considered seabirds, swallows take up residence in the oceanside cliffs. Unlike gulls, they are rarely seen except in flight, and while airborne their little wings are in almost perpetual motion. Their frantic motions were a pleasure to watch, but their most remarkable aerial stunts came on those rare occasions when they would cease flapping to catch an updraft. Then, black wings tucked back, white bellies showing, they would sail through the air looking every bit like miniature killer whales—tiny Shamus and "free" Willies—being swept along on currents of wind. (Almost as neat as its winning ways is the bank swallow's scientific name: *Riparia riparia.*)

The beach widened again, and in the distance I saw people, which meant there must be a hollow ahead. My mind was packing up and preparing for landfall when suddenly a number of simultaneous occurrences yanked my attention back to the beach and capped the day's beach portion of the excursion as it had commenced, in breathtaking fashion.

Only a few dozen yards ahead a great blue heron, well out of its usual haunts, rose up, lumbered into flight, and began to swoop straight at me, for all I knew intending to snatch and spirit me away. With its huge wingspan, long skinny neck, and protuberant beak, the heron might have been a pterodactyl, and for a fantastic moment I was frozen in place, awestruck and gripped by a feeling like Beston's ancient terror. Only when it cleared my head by inches did I relax, but before I could recover my wits fully I noticed what seemed to be sea creatures breaching a couple of hundred yards off the beach. To my amazement, whales were breaking the surface every few seconds—dazzling white whales, a whole pod of them, in a show that could have been either Captain Ahab's dream come true or his worst nightmare.

The heron was real, but the white whales . . . getting a grip, I realized what was actually happening: the sun had come out from under cover for the first time all day, and the late slanting rays were brilliantly illuminating waves breaking over the outer bars. My white whales were in fact sunlit whitecaps. Although I think I have a fairly vivid and inventive mind, I consider myself rationally grounded on the whole, and so the ability of this place to sweep me up into flights of fancy instantly, especially when the walk was threatening to hit a wall of routine, left me both stunned and delighted; my imagination, I was pleased to discover, was alive and well.

At this same moment I sensed all sorts of change beginning to take place in front of me. For one thing, the beach no longer pointed down Maine—the Cape's westward trend was at last not just intuited, it was perceptible, undeniable. Then I noticed the first houses since Coast Guard Beach. Civilization.

There were a few strollers, but mostly fishermen on the public beach (known as Maguire's Landing Beach, at Le Count's Hollow). Each angler had two or three rods stuck in the sand, and all were standing around schmoozing. A few dogfish carcasses littered the sand, and only one fisherman had landed a prize, a striped bass. As I eyed the dying striper, unceremoniously plopped on the beach, its owner walked over to me and said, somewhat defensively, "It's legal—right on the nose." In death's throes the magnificent game fish was just a shadow of its former self, its signature bright colors fading, fading, with each weakened, futile flap of sand-encrusted gills.

Another fisherman told me it was going on to seven o'clock. I decided to leave the beach here, for Wellfleet center was a couple of miles away, and the more ground I could cover on pavement, the quicker I'd get there. In addition, muscle fatigue was setting in. H.T. battled chronic illness much of his adult life before succumbing to tuberculosis, "consumption," at age forty-four. Nevertheless, he also enjoyed periods of great vitality, his endurance strengthened by daily four-hour walks. I'd covered approximately the same ground as Thoreau and Channing had on Day One, 1849—Orleans to Wellfleet—and came away from the beach with a newfound respect for the plucky constitutions of the men from Concord, who did all right for themselves even without the benefit of Nautilus machines and step aerobics.

The Cape Cod National Seashore is unique in that it was the first national park proposed to be established on land not already under federal ownership. The Seashore legislation (enacted by President Kennedy on August 7, 1961) gave existing homeowners a number of options for holding on to or disposing of their property (including selling to the government outright), provided the property was of "the same nature and quality" it had been on September 1, 1959, the year the bill was first filed. This retroactive cutoff date was designed to discourage speculation and to prevent individuals from inflating market value and profiting excessively at Uncle Sam's expense by turning cottages into palazzos before offering them up to the Park Service. As a result of the legislation's stipulations and subsequent strict zoning regulations, the Seashore's few residential enclaves are communities frozen in time. Emerging from the relative wildness of Thoreau's Cape Cod at Maguire's Landing, I felt that I had been fast-forwarded into the twentieth century, but not all the way—this is Cape Cod as it looked at the dawn of Camelot.

Situated along one of the world's most spectacular shorelines, the first cottages I came across were modest in the extreme, almost endearingly tacky, built in the style of those flimsy bungalows found in unfashionable Florida retirement communities. They were like comfort food for the eyes, faithful to my unadulterated memories of a simpler Cape, simpler times, and I was glad for the sight of them—after the beach I wanted to ease my way back to modernity slowly.

The boxy cottages, sided in faded pastels the colors of assorted Necco wafers, are situated in a pine grove at the head of aptly named Ocean View Drive, which runs parallel to the shore. Farther up on Ocean View are more traditional cottages, casual cabins the locals call "sweep-outs" because of their easygoing maintenance needs—anything more than a once-over with a broom is wasted motion.

One cottage in particular caught my eye, for it was my dream house, repository of youth and innocence, my life's one constant material desire. Could I not stay young forever if I possessed such a place? "Perhaps what most moves us in winter is some reminiscence of far-off summer," wrote Thoreau. Set on a rise overlooking an open plain stretching to the beach, the sweep-out was a study in artful simplicity with its weathered shingles, chipping white shutters, and "yard" consisting of six blades of beach grass and tottering carousel clothesline. From the road I could almost hear the *thwack* of its screen door slamming, and I just knew the cozy interior harbored one of summer's great smells, that oddly agreeable, irradicable odor of must and mildew peculiar to cottages shuttered for nine months of the year.

A number of other beach houses were scattered about on both

sides of Ocean View. A few more were of the flat-roofed, studio variety; others, though larger and featuring more contemporary touches than the sweep-outs, still bore allegiance to the spare, functional Cape Cod style.

The Seashore took over before large-scale development established a beachhead on the Atlantic side, and beyond the parking lot at White Crest Beach the small clusters of oceanfront and oceanview homes petered out, giving way to a landscape thick with scrub trees, dune plants, and heavy brush. I could hear loud music coming from down near the beach and figured some kids were hanging out in the dunes with a boom box. There below, where Cahoon Hollow opens to the ocean, I spied the true source of the tunes: the Beachcomber, the only bar located directly on the outer beach, cooking for the Labor Day weekend.

The building housing the Beachcomber was at one time among the outer beach's numerous Coast Guard Life Saving Stations, which beginning in 1872 rendered Humane houses obsolete. (Thoreau would have been pleased.) After a grinding hike over sand, the Beachcomber sure looked like a humane house to me, a real lifesaver.

In *Cape Cod* H.T. speaks in a disapproving tone of the tourist who "thinks more of the wine than the brine." I'm admittedly one who's partial to both the wine-dark sea and the cordial juice, the aqua and the aqua vitae, and I seriously considered descending into the Hollow to have a drink and then grab a cab to town later. At the Beachcomber I could sit on the deck, relax, have a few shrimp from the outdoor grill. The beach volleyball games would be breaking up soon; perhaps some of the players might join me for a libation, and I'd regale them with tales of great blue herons and illusory white whales.

Trying to come to a decision, I let my gaze drift over the Beachcomber's roof to the vast sea beyond, turned sapphirine in the sharp late light. How peaceful it was, but early evening's serenity in no way masked the ocean's mighty nature or made me forget its predilection for the tempest. H.T. commented that "this same placid Ocean, as civil now as a city's harbor . . . will erelong be lashed in a sudden fury, and all its caves and cliffs will resound with tumult." The resident of inland Concord highly recommended approaching these shores in stormy weather, but I didn't feel shortchanged by the mild conditions—I've seen storms before, plenty of them.

As I watched the ocean slowly and evenly heave up and down, like a blanket pulled over a slumbering giant having sweet dreams, I suddenly remembered that I didn't have a place to sleep that night. My lodging needs helped me make up my mind about my next move, and with a little regret I turned from the Beachcomber and started across the Cape for town.

Wellfleet Village

KAROL B. WYCKOFF

4

The Wellfleet Oystermen

One of the most attractive points for visitors

is in the northeast part of Wellfleet, where

accommodations (I mean for men and

women of tolerable health and habits) could

probably be had within half a

mile of the seashore.

CAPE COD

Evening shade had lowered over the western sky nearly to treetop level, leaving just a crack through which the squinting sun stole one last peek east. Only steps away from the beach the trees grew much taller, and the forested road darkened quickly as daylight took its leave. Carloads of people were coming to and from the Beachcomber, those departing heading out on my side of the winding road. America was behind me again—with designated drivers at the wheel, I hoped.

I was on Cahoon Hollow Road, which like most lanes on the

ocean side is laid out roughly east to west, running perpendicular to both the beach and the main trunk road, Route 6. The surrounding woods were empty but for swarms of hungry mosquitoes, which proceeded to make a meal of me. I pulled on sweatpants and a light jacket and made a mental note: *Buy insect repellent.*

The first landmark I came upon was Great Pond, one of the Cape's numerous kettle ponds. Vestiges of glacial melting, kettle ponds are well named—I looked down on Great Pond from a rim perhaps fifty feet above the water's surface. This body of water is about half a mile south of Williams Pond, near where Thoreau and Channing stayed the first night in 1849 with John Newcomb, an elderly Wellfleet oysterman, "the merriest old man that we had ever seen," who entertained and regaled them with stories well into the evening. (Newcomb was eighty-eight when they visited; Thoreau took him for sixty or seventy. Later he would think a sixty-year-old lighthouse keeper forty. So much for the old salt stereotype.)

As I turned to leave, a light came on in a home on the opposite shore, its beam flickering across the pond. I stopped and watched it, transfixed, like Gatsby staring at the beacon on Daisy's dock, and suddenly had an unexplainable urge to go to its source, wanting badly to know who lived there, what they were doing, and if I might join them. The moment passed slowly. How is it that light cast over darkened waters can pierce the heart like a laser, and bore into that chamber where deep longing dwells?

After Great Pond the road came to a fork, and I actually took the correct turn. Soon I could hear the sounds of cars zipping by. There was Route 6, and a convenience store of a well-known chain. *Real* civilization.

I was quite familiar with the general area, but coming here by the all-beach route had knocked me somewhat off my bearings. I knew there were roadside motels in the vicinity, but I couldn't gauge exactly how close. It's a whole new ballgame when you're hoofing it; a motel five minutes by car could take an hour to reach by foot, and I wasn't up for much more hiking. At the convenience store I asked the young woman behind the counter if there were any motels within reasonable walking distance. The ensuing dialogue went something like this:

"Sorry, I can't do that."

"Can't do what?"

"We're not supposed to recommend places to stay. Company policy."

"Recommend? I just want to know where, how far, that's all. I'm not looking for a recommendation."

"Can't do it."

"Tell you what," I said, trying to remain calm, "you don't have to say a word, just point. Can you do that for me, please? Just point—now, am I better off going north or south?"

"Sorry," she said, firmly and unapologetically, turning to fiddle with the cigarette display.

Biting my tongue, I walked out the door. I wanted to keep my mood upbeat after a pleasant day playing nature boy, and I wasn't about to let this encounter with a member of my own species bring me down.

I decided to go straight to town, where I was sure—well, almost sure—I'd find a room. After making a dangerous crossing of Route 6, I came upon an inn. It was out of my price range, but like Kerouac's literary alter ego Sal Paradise in *On the Road*, who reluctantly shelled out for a bus ticket and abandoned his dream of hitchhiking West when he got stuck on an upstate New York road to nowhere, I was ready to bust my budget to get a bed on the first night. Unfortunately, there was no room at the inn until Monday, the clerk informed me, but she did so graciously, and I left feeling better. I kept going in the direction of Wellfleet center, passing a couple of art galleries, including one doubling as a restaurant. Nowhere to be found on East Main were the cozy inns and B&Bs I'd visualized, and I was beginning to suspect that they were the products of wishful thinking.

The homes on the outskirts of town were mostly dark and looked uninhabited, but there was a steady flow of traffic. With growing panic I noticed that a majority of the cars bore license plates embossed with a rendering of the Statue of Liberty. Where New Yorkers go, "No Vacancy" signs are sure to follow.

Conventional wisdom had always held that the Cape was less crowded over Labor Day than on the other big summer holidays because people stayed home getting the kids ready for school, and I'd been confident that I'd have little difficulty securing a bed. I was coming to realize just how outmoded my thinking had been; perhaps I'd done too many Labor Day business reports from motel-glutted Hyannis. My usually reliable instincts had failed to alert me that Wellfleet had become quite trendy with the disposable income crowd, and that the kind of people who came here weren't the type for whom back-to-school sales were a priority. I'd been foolish not to make prior arrangements. So much for spontaneity.

I walked by an old house set right on the sidewalk and lingered a second to eavesdrop. Inside, three couples my age were grouped around a large table enjoying dinner by candlelight. Tall, elegant champagne flutes reflected the candles' glow, and the sparkling wine shimmered rosily, like a tincture of Cape Cod Bay sunset captured in crystal. I was tempted to knock on the door and ask if I could join them. After all, H.T. had knocked on Wellfleet doors until Newcomb took him and Channing in; might I not do the same? Although the idea intrigued and amused me, I was too fainthearted to follow through. In the middle of town I found a pay phone and started calling every B&B in the phone book. And struck out. Since I'd not yet become desperate or courageous enough to beg for a couch or a porch hammock, I called motels on Route 6. How would I get out there? Cab. I looked up taxi companies in the Yellow Pages. There was no cab service in Wellfleet (good thing I'd not tarried at the Beachcomber). Well, I could always thumb, and called the motels anyway. Nada. Without exception the motel clerks were surly, suspicious ("A single? One night? Whaddaya mean you're *walking?*"), and contemptuously incredulous, making me feel that in calling I'd committed an unbelievable faux pas, like asking directions for the bridge to Martha's Vineyard or something equally yokel. In contrast, the bed and breakfast folks were warm and friendly, some sounding almost saddened they couldn't take me in.

A number of B&B owners suggested an inn near the harbor, where hospitality industry scuttlebutt had it that there were some openings, and I decided to head that way.

It took me about ten seconds to exit Wellfleet center, quite possibly the smallest contiguous downtown on the entire Cape, not lengthy enough to host even a traffic light. Size might be its saving grace — despite Wellfleet's artsy/literary reputation and predominantly affluent summer crowd, its downtown has been able to stave off gentrification because there simply isn't room enough for it to go precious. There are no boutiques here boasting branches in Palm Beach and La Jolla; Wellfleet center's core function, as a consultant might phrase it, is to provide just the basic necessities of human commerce. There's Town Hall, a pharmacy, a newsstand, a package store, a little T-shirt shop, a ticket kiosk for the local theatrical troupe, a townie-flavored eatery, and that's pretty much it. The one exception to the center's sumptuary laws: a coat-and-tie restaurant suitable for wining and dining favored company. The west end of the tiny business district is anchored by a Roman Catholic church—staples for the soul—the east end by little Lema's Market, a throwback to the days of the old neighborhood A&P, right down to keeping what must be the 1990s retail equivalent of bankers' hours.

Wellfleet's appealing points were totally lost on me this evening, however, caught up as I was in the hunt for a place to lay my head. I set my sights on the harbor district, where I ran into flocks of young teens hanging out, flirting and having a grand time doing nothing much. Scrubbed clean after a day at the beach, these golden children of summer reminded me . . . of *me,* thirty years ago, although it was not possible that I was ever as unself-conscious as these kids appeared to be.

No vacancy, a clerk with a British accent told me upon arrival at the inn, they'd just given the last room away. The inn's owner gave me a few names of places he thought might have a spare bed. Could I use his phone? "There's a public phone back in town," he replied. On any other occasion I would probably find a small town with no taxis and one pay phone charming, but by now Wellfleet was really starting to irritate me.

On the spot I decided to sleep on the Atlantic beach. The prospect didn't faze me much, for the evening felt warm. True, H.T. never slept on the beach when he traveled the Cape, believing that a long day's journey had earned him the right to a soft bed. Although I agreed, at nine o'clock on this Labor Day Saturday I had run out of options.

Only one thing gave me pause: I had to maneuver my way back to the beach over dark, twisty Cahoon Hollow Road. My concern was less with mosquitoes, skunks, and drunk drivers than with the ever-vigilant Cape Cod police. Sleeping is banned on Cape beaches, and cops enforce the law with great zeal. They seem to have especially sensitive antennae for beach-bound lovers, as I first discovered during summer vacations from college; I used to think it might be easier to infiltrate the Kennedy compound than to slip by the constabulary unobserved to pursue *l'amore* in the privacy of the dunes.

Even going solo, as I was now, I'd likely be stopped and questioned before reaching the beach. Almost everyone else in Wellfleet seemed to be in a surly mood tonight, and I wasn't expecting the cops to be any different. Then again, a night in jail might not be such a bad idea—at least I'd have a place to stay. Didn't H.T. spend one famous night in the Concord slammer, protesting the Mexican war and slavery? I could walk into the Wellfleet police station and declare: "You must incarcerate me, Sergeant! I refuse to pay the poll tax!" The chief of police is said to be a man of letters (an ex–New York cop who writes mystery novels— Wellfleet's a regular Cabot Cove); perhaps the chief would be sympathetic.

Hunger was making me a little punchy, and I decided to grab some dinner before attempting the beach; if I couldn't have a warm bed I'd at least have a square meal. The Wellfleet Oyster House looked inviting, and luckily there was no dress code. "Welcome," said the accommodating hostess in a warm Irish brogue. "Sit anywhere."

The structure housing the restaurant was built in 1750. With the help of dim lighting and some strategically placed period pieces, The Oyster House invoked the look and ambiance of a colonial tavern, and it required no great leap of imagination to picture King George's outer Cape subjects gathered here to talk a little treason.

I chose to sit in the cozy bar, where a friendly bartender served me food and drink. With a glass of the cordial juice in hand, I found Wellfleet instantly more attractive. The Oyster House was unusually quiet for a holiday weekend in a sold-out town, almost dead, but it could have had nothing to do with the food, which was delicious.

With time on her hands, the bartender began to make conversation. To my surprise, she was fascinated that I was walking the outer beach; I'd assumed would-be Thoreaus came trooping through here regularly. But what really floored her was my answer to her inevitable follow-up question: "Where are you staying tonight?"

"Nowhere, I don't have a place."

In moments word had spread among the staff that a guy at the bar was hiking from Orleans to Provincetown, didn't have a place to stay for the night, and was thinking of sleeping on the beach. Soon I was surrounded by curious waitresses, bus help, the hostess, and even the chef. No one could believe there were no vacancies in Wellfleet, which made me feel not such an idiot for failing to book a reservation.

The bartender phoned many of the same places I'd called earlier. Shaking her head after the umpteenth rejection, she said, "It hasn't been this busy on Labor Day since I can remember." She and her husband would be happy to have me stay in their guest room, she told me, but they lived in Brewster, too far in the opposite direction.

The helpful group at the bar had been joined by a young dishwasher, who said he was positive a motel near his house in North Truro had a vacancy. Not only that, but he offered to take me there.

"I'm meeting some friends next door to the motel for a few

beers and to shoot some pool anyway . . . say, why don't you join us after you get your room?" he asked.

Beers? Billiards? *And* a bed? "You're on, brother," I told my benefactor, whose name was Richard.

After a quick phone call, I found myself committed to two nights at a place in North Truro. That arrangement would disrupt the walk's linear progression, but North Truro was centrally located for accomplishing most of my goals, and now I had a guarantee of weekend shelter.

I bought a round of drinks for the staff, and then there were waves good-bye at the restaurant door, and cries of "Come back and tell us how the trip went!" Outside, Richard and I were joined by his friend Greg, also a dishwasher, a man about my age wearing a seventies-style John Davidson haircut. The three of us climbed into Richard's car, a pre–oil embargo American bomber of indeterminate make. I got in the back seat, which had no upholstery, just the exposed steel well, but I maneuvered my rear into a semi-comfortable position and felt as if I were in a Rolls Royce.

As he warmed up the old clunker, Richard asked about my walk. I told him and handed him a copy of *Cape Cod* from my backpack. He looked it over with help from a beam emanating from a restaurant window, for his car's dome light didn't work. "Henry David Thoreau . . . doesn't he live on the Cape?"

Greg spoke up first. "No, Thoreau lived and died over a hundred years ago," he said softly.

"Oh yeah, I was thinking of someone else."

"Maybe Alexander Theroux," I said. "I think he lives in Dennis."

Richard continued thumbing through *Cape Cod*. He stopped

abruptly at the heading for Chapter 5. "Listen, Greg! *The Wellfleet Oysterman!*" Turning to me, he exclaimed excitedly: "That's *us*! Me and Greg—*we're* Wellfleet oystermen!"

It was so. Besides washing dishes in two local restaurants, banging nails, and taking on whatever other odd jobs came about, Richard and his pal also harvested oysters (and quahogs, the up-and-coming crop) in Wellfleet Harbor. They'd be out there tomorrow, Richard said, working for a man who farmed the flats using the latest aquaculture techniques.

This was a most serendipitous development. H.T.'s account of spending a night with John Newcomb, the Wellfleet oysterman, makes for *Cape Cod*'s most entertaining chapter, and now I'd met my own shellfishermen. "Thank you," I said silently to my guardian angel.

Mufflerless, the car gunned out onto Route 6. Like old John Newcomb, young Richard liked to talk, and other than occasionally sprinkling his conversation with slang, he was quite articulate. "Yup, I'm a native," he declared proudly, the scion of an old, old Wellfleet family, though he was now renting a house in Truro. Adhering to an ancient family tradition, he said, he'd just been inducted into the Masons, having recently reached his twenty-first birthday. As he informed me of this there was such a glow to his face that for a moment I thought the overhead light was working again. Obviously, becoming a Mason was a high point of his tender years, and seeing as I don't know any Masons, I told him it was an honor to make one's acquaintance.

"No Masons in Boston?" he asked.

"Not that I'm aware of," I replied. "Lots of Knights of Columbus, though."

Richard had tried a year of pharmacy college in Boston after Nauset Regional High School, didn't like the city one bit, and was hoping to resume his studies and get an associate's degree one of these days at the 4 Cs—Cape Cod Community College. It was a familiar tale of a fish out of water, and I'd heard it often. All over the world rural youth are flocking to big cities, but for some reason young Cape Codders find the transition to urban life particularly difficult. For some, making the journey off-Cape is like going to a foreign country—and indeed, as Thoreau once pointed out, even by the short route over water, Provincetown and the Lower Cape are twice as far from Boston as England is from France. The overland route to the capital city can be especially daunting; going "up" to the canal, and then "up" to Boston can seem truly uphill from down here.

Greg, who had been quiet until now, asked me what I did for a living. When I told him I worked for a state senator, he immediately wanted to know how she stood on labor issues. This can be a tricky question on the Cape, so I hesitated before answering cautiously, "She's a friend of the working man."

"I used to work for the union back home," he went on, mentioning another New England state. "I was an organizer."

"So why'd you move here?"

"Got in a little trouble, had to leave."

A jumble of images flashed through my tired, overripe mind: picket lines, charging Pinkertons, bloody truncheons, broken heads. "Trouble with the union?" I asked in a whisper, afraid I might be touching on a sensitive subject.

Greg gave me a smile over his shoulder. "You could say that, I guess—my marriage broke up. *That* union. So I came here, about five years ago, to live as the Cape Codders live, peaceably by the sea, to fish a little, and to rake oysters. That's my story."

He delivered this statement in his sincere, rumbling bass, and I found myself unexpectedly moved, as if he'd said something quite profound, although after reading *Cape Cod* I shouldn't have been greatly surprised by the simple eloquence of a Wellfleet oysterman.

Richard continued to chatter on; this junior oysterman was also capable of coming up with an occasional pearl. With the aplomb of a scholar who's studied the matter at length, he informed me that Lower Cape Codders born east of Route 6, the ocean side, tend to be moody, simmering individuals prone to sudden wild outbursts, while those born west of 6 reflect the more pacific nature of the nearby bay. It made sense to me, but Greg wasn't buying it. "What about that guy Smith?" he demanded. "He's lived all his life in that shack by the harbor, and he's *dangerous*!"

"Exception that proves the rule?" I offered.

We pulled into the parking lot shared by my motel and Goody Hallett's, a bar. After I registered, the oystermen dropped me off at my room. Over his protests, I pressed twenty bucks on Richard for his help getting me a room, and for gas; I figured his tank had guzzled an amount worth at least half that much going the eight miles from Wellfleet center to North Truro.

Five minutes later I entered Goody Hallett's, a sprawling, barnlike place that was nearly empty. In back of the room, about half a mile away, I spotted my companions at the pool tables, and joined them. They were with their buddies, a friendly, easygoing bunch, a few locals and some vacationing college kids in no apparent rush to be back at school even though it was course registration week. (I could relate.) Richard bought me a beer, and the players generously yielded the table to their guest of honor. "Rack 'em up," I said.

The game was eight ball. Perhaps a day on the beach had sharpened my reflexes, because I proceeded to run the table, my winning repertoire including a couple of very pretty combo shots and even one intricate bank job. After burying the last ball in a corner pocket, I looked up in triumph only to see that everyone was staring at me, intently. I sure hoped all the local boys had been born on the Bay side. One of the bigger fellows came over and slapped me on the shoulder. "What are you, some city slicker come down to hustle us poor country boys?" And then he let out a huge laugh.

They all joined in, and so did I. And why not? The only stakes were the cost of the next game, paid for by the loser. The players had been a little taken aback by my billiard skills, that's all. I'm really no pool shark; I just happened to be lucky tonight. Nevertheless, to make sure there were no lingering doubts I announced loudly, "If I have a few more beers my game will go right to hell." I did, and it did.

Mark Twain poked fun at his Grand Touring countrymen in *The Innocents Abroad,* but I showed it's possible to be a naïf traveling right in my own backyard. *Cape Cod* and *On The Road* were my Baedekers, not *Easy Rider.* It hadn't occurred to me until after I'd polished off the table that I was a stranger in the back room of a saloon on an isolated rural road, surrounded by drinking men with cue sticks in their hands, and whipping them at pool on their turf as blithely as if I were down my own cellar with old pals. In fact, the men were good, generous souls without a hint of mean-ness about them, but I couldn't help speculating on what could have happened tonight with a different, less friendly cast of char-acters.

Back-to-back losses got me bumped from the table. Richard, Greg, and I retired to drink and talked until past midnight, mostly about the oyster trade.

I was familiar with some of the history of Wellfleet oystering from H.T.'s examination of the topic in *Cape Cod.* The principles of aquaculture so highly touted today are really nothing new, for both immature and full-grown oysters have been "bedded" in Wellfleet waters to attain "the proper relish of Billingsgate" for over two centuries. Thoreau reported that native oysters died out here around 1770, for reasons unknown. Such a mysterious plague today would no doubt be ascribed to man's doings; colonial Wellfleeters believed the oysters' disappearance was God's punishment for quarreling over the harvest with neighboring towns.

The aquaculturists sowing and reaping in present-day Wellfleet have updated the old methods, but it's all still pretty low-tech. Grown mainly from seed, young shellfish propagate in metal cages or wooden boxes placed on the harbor bottom, the containers covered with mesh to thwart predators. The boxes are exposed at low tide, deliberately, for until the oyster and quahog crops reach marketable maturity they require much tending by man or machine. At high tide the shellfish grants are marked off by prominent orange buoys. Richard informed me that aquafarming had earned the ire of some waterfront property owners, upset with the increased activity within direct view of their homes. One big sticking point was the fact that most oystermen drove the beach to reach their grants. There'd been endless meetings about the new methods of shellfishing, he said; a couple of homeowners had even brought suit.

Despite their differences, modern Cape Codders have demonstrated a surprising knack for getting along by observing the sensible Yankee "live and let live" philosophy of human relations. However, when perceived threats to the "divine right" of property are involved, all bets are off, and out come the committees, the petitions, and the lawyers. Its citizens proclaim great love and concern for the Cape, but too often real interest ends at the property line, or extends only as far as the eye can see. It's of little consequence to the complainers that aquaculture's boom has revived a traditional, natural Cape Cod industry; to them, the main thing is that it "spoils the view."

Finally, it came time to take my leave of the convivial company. Richard shook my hand and, meaning it as the supreme compliment said, "You're the mellowest person from Boston I ever met." He invited me back to his house to continue the party and even crash on a couch if I wanted to, but though H.T. claimed that the "fisherman's hut is the true hotel," I declined. Like Newcomb, who went to bed only reluctantly after a rousing evening's conversation with Thoreau and Channing, Richard looked good for a few more hours, and I really needed to get some sleep.

Thoreau and Channing had been kept well entertained by their oysterman, who offered them a slice of Cape Cod life, and I felt my new acquaintances had acquitted themselves well in this regard. I lifted my bottle of Bud Light, and groped for words to toast them by. "To the Wellfleet Oystermen: thanks for your help and hospitality. Remember, the *world's* your oyster, and, ah, may you open it with your swords." I had butchered the Bard brutally, but the assembled responded with war whoops and rebel yells anyway.

Back in my room, I stayed up a while making some notes. It was difficult to believe that I'd arrived in Orleans little over twelve hours before. "You've had quite a day," I said to myself, unconsciously using an expression from childhood that had been my parents' unmistakable signal for me to go to bed. I put my notebook down and turned out the light. A bed had never felt better. Yes, I'd had quite a day.

KAROL B. WYCKOFF

5

Highland Light to Race Point: The Long March

Before we left the light-house we were obliged

to annoint our shoes faithfully with tallow,

for walking on the beach, in the salt water

and sand, had turned them red and crisp.

CAPE COD

I. Highland Light

 A few hours later, I was up. North Truro was socked in with fog and mist, and I put off a trip to the beach to watch the sunrise *à la* Thoreau, the pea soup buying me some welcome sack time. I awoke again after a short nap much refreshed, and hungry as a horse. Goody Hallett's looked like the kind of place that served a hearty fisherman's breakfast, and I went over. Closed, said a sign. Open at four.

There was no other restaurant nearby, but I recalled that the motel's night desk clerk had mentioned something about a "continental" breakfast. unfortunately, by the time i got to the motel office, I found only some crumbs and jelly smears on a paper-lined tray. There was a half a cup left in a Mister Coffee on a side table; the clerk behind the desk watched me pour, not offering to make another pot.

Nothing could bother me this morning, however, and I left the office and hit Route 6 with a spring in my step. Facing the day, its choices and possibilities, I was as happy as I'd been in years, almost giddily so. The only problem confronting me was which way to go.

I was beginning my second day where H.T. had begun his third in 1849; the automobile trip to North Truro had opened an eight-mile gap in my walking itinerary, the stretch of beach from Cahoon Hollow to Highland Light. To retrace those steps from north to south, ending up back in Wellfleet, far from my motel, seemed not only inefficient but also went against the grain of H.T.'s premier walk. I decided instead to set out from nearby Highland Light and make my way to Race Point and into Provincetown. By now it was obvious I'd underestimated the time needed to complete my task; a return trip would be necessary. This gave me a perfect excuse to take another long three-day weekend walking the outer beach, and the prospect of coming back over Columbus Day lifted my spirits even further. There may be a method to my madness after all.

I set off briskly on Route 6 through North Truro, the rolling, windswept moorlands leaving no question that I'd reached the beginning of land's end. At the road to Highland Light I turned east, where before me the sun was attempting to burn through a lingering mist. Larger and larger it grew in the sky, a ruby red circle shining through a veil of vapor; I felt I could almost reach out and touch it. But then the fog gathered again, thick as flannel, and the sun receded until it was tiny, round, and silver as a dime; finally it disappeared altogether. How had the hot star failed to scorch away morning's grayness? The sea mists may have looked ethereal, but their hold on the day was tenacious.

It was one of those airless summer days that settles over the Cape on occasion, and even the Atlantic sea breeze had succumbed to a general lassitude. It was also quite muggy, and I was working up a good sweat when Highland Light loomed up before me at the edge of the sea cliff. In the lighthouse's parking lot stood what appeared from a distance to be a portable refreshment stand, and I hastened to it hungrily and thirstily.

It was no refreshment stand, but rather a mobile booth set up by a local resident to alert the public to Highland's impending demise. At the time cliffside Highland Light was in grave danger of being lost to erosion, and with the Interior Department and the Coast Guard still dithering over plans and payment for a lifesaving move, it was left to citizen activists to keep the government's feet to the fire. As most readers familiar with the Cape are no doubt aware, it had become necessary to move the lighthouse (also known as Cape Cod Light) back from the bank to save it. Engineering for the move had to be completed before the bluff was 100 feet from the tower, and with that limit nearly reached on the day in question, alarmed advocates feared the window of opportunity was about to close forever.

"Move It or Lose It!" read a board nailed to the little trailer. I approached and began a conversation with the friendly older fellow manning the booth, a member of the Save the Lighthouse Committee. He told me that each lighthouse that has stood here, beginning with the original 1797 structure, has been at approximately the same site—even though the effects of erosion must have been clear long ago. He asked me to sign a petition and make a donation to the cause. I did both, but with some irritation that it took such a grass-roots effort to get the government to act. As the committee's typewritten brochure makes clear, "This *is* Cape Cod's Light." Thankfully, the government finally got on with the job, saving this towering icon to our seafaring heritage in the nick of time.

Thoreau was enchanted by this location. He made friends with the lighthouse keepers, stayed here in 1849 and on subsequent visits, and witnessed construction of the present tower during his final trip in 1857.

He likened the view from Highland Light to that from a vessel, "the masthead of a man-of-war, 30 miles at sea." Surveys from this high point on the Cape's narrow extremity are still outstanding, though probably not as sweeping as those Thoreau experienced. Unfortunately, the erosion problems keep people from taking full opportunity of the vantage point at the bank's edge beyond the lighthouse, while views to the west of the bay and Provincetown are somewhat obstructed by foliage, telephone wires, and the old hotel that now houses the Historical Museum. Nonetheless, Highland remains the best "scenic overlook" that I know on Cape Cod.

I left Highland Light and stopped in at the nearby little nine-hole Highland Links, whose seventh fairway would become the ultimate resting spot for the lighthouse upon its relocation in 1996 (prompting wags to make an oxymoronic observation that Highland Links would now resemble the world's largest miniature golf course). There was a snack bar at the pro shop, and I took my meal on the deck while watching golfers chip up to the nearby green. I dined on the house specialty—hot dogs, four to be exact; after all, I hadn't breakfasted and had miles to go before I would eat . . . again.

II. Head of the Meadow

Below Highland Light a road leads directly to the outer beach but, preoccupied, I overlooked it. Instead I headed back to Route 6 via Highland Road and thence to the beach called Head of the Meadow, a time-consuming trek that left me bathed in sweat. Narrow Truro is commonly referred to as the Cape's "wrist"; today it might have been Atlas's wrist. Walking gave me a new perspective of the landmass and distances, and my old familiar Cape Cod had greatly expanded. Little matter, as I was in an expansive mood, already convinced that touring the Cape by foot is the best way to go, impractical as that would be for most people.

Winding through a forest where pine and oak battle for scrubby supremacy, Head of the Meadow Road is one of those chunky, rough-surfaced Cape Cod byways that look as if they were paved by Nestlé rather than by the D.P.W. Ahead a station wagon with a rack of bikes on top had pulled over onto the sandy shoulder, and as I walked by, the occupants and I exchanged greetings.

They were a family of four from the midwest, and for some unfathomable reason they wanted to park out in the woods and bike the final quarter of a mile to Head of the Meadow, where there is not only parking but also an entryway to a fine bike path. Kids and parents alike were so excited by the prospect of riding down to the beach in style—it was as if they had driven 1,200 miles solely for this purpose—that I tried to let them down gently.

"You know, the government doesn't like competition, and I've seen 'No Parking' signs around, and, well . . . look, I think you'll get the hook."

Even as I was giving my spiel the father started unloading

bikes from the roof. He had decided to risk it, he said, and we parted with mutual good wishes and no hard feelings. Their license plate indicated they were from the "Show Me" state, and I thought that in due time a park ranger or Truro cop would be only too happy to oblige and show Dad the best bike route to the Provincetown tow lot.

I arrived at Head of the Meadow, one of the beaches along the National Seashore whose administration is divided between the town and the Park Service. The sun had finally won its tug of war with the clouds, and the beach was getting crowded. Small breakers sparkled in the bright light, and a part of me just wanted to stay put and stretch out on the sand.

I took off my sneakers and started schlepping, right away getting an unpleasant surprise—going barefoot on abrasive sand the day before had opened a couple of cuts between the toes on both my feet, thin and nasty, like paper cuts. With every step the wounds were rubbed raw, and I felt as if I were walking on razor blades. I put my Reeboks back on, but the heavy sand restricted my progress; at this rate I'd get to Provincetown by Memorial Day.

So I went barefoot again, plodding on like the religious pilgrims who endure bloody feet to climb rocky Croagh Patrick Mountain in Ireland, accepting my pain and offering it up for the souls in purgatory. This, then, would be my penance for imagining that I could so lightly gambol in the true Atlantic City.

Those bound for Provincetown by the beach route will find that the sea cliff, and thus that part of the outer Cape whose genesis is glacial, essentially ends at Head of the Meadow. From here on in, the curling strip of Cape is known to geologists as the Provincetown or Provincelands Spit, formed in postglacial times by longshore currents carrying eroded deposits away from the marine scarp (a process that is ongoing). The deposits' buildup here gives the bared and bended arm its fist.

The difference in topography is immediately noticeable. From the gravel and clay cliffs of Eastham and Wellfleet, the landscape changes markedly to one dominated by an overlay of powdery sand softer and whiter than on other parts of the outer beach. Wrenched from the cliffs, pounded over an eon on the beach by waves, moved northward by currents sometimes wild, sometimes benign, the sand on the spit has been milled to a consistency that locals commonly call "sugar sand."

A barrier wall remains between beach and hinterland, and though made mainly of sand it's a formidable replacement for the earthen cliff, fifty feet or so high and sheer, nearly impossible to climb and tall enough to block the view beyond. At some points erosion has taken large mouthfuls out of the sand barrier, fully exposing gnarled roots of low, brambly vegetation above and giving the dune top the look of a Florida mangrove swamp gone high and dry.

A quarter of a mile beyond Head of the Meadow, past a few sunbathers who had distanced themselves from the crowd, the beach was empty again, empty not only of humans but of other creatures, at least for the time being—not even a gull was in sight. But evidence of recent gatherings of species was strewn about everywhere, including broken seashells and stripped carcasses of skates and dogfish, no doubt the handiwork of shore birds, as well as unmistakable tracks and droppings of *Homo sapiens*: dozens of Styrofoam cups and empty beer cans lay discarded over a wide area. The shore was not a tenth as littered as most urban beaches and parks, but even so, the thoughtlessness of those who had come to this special place and abused the privilege upset and angered me.

When I was a kid in school, a popular imperative was: "Don't be a litterbug." That might have been an innocuous pitch for the environment during an era of silent springs, but at least there was an emphasis on personal responsibility and respect for the immediate space around you. Now the buzzphrase is the more abstract "save the planet," an unassailably high-minded yet ultimately hollow expression. The kids who had made such a mess on the beach near Head of the Meadow (given the remote location and volume of garbage, the polluters almost certainly were young people) are of the first generation to come of age since the inception of Earth Day, the first truly "green" generation, indoctrinated since kindergarten with an environmental manifesto, ready to go forth and "save the planet." Tell me: where exactly do they think this planet begins?

It was amazing to me that a place of such obvious activity, human and otherwise, was empty in the middle of day. Have you ever frequented a restaurant for lunch that's always so quiet you wonder how the place stays in business? Then you get your answer one evening when you go for dinner and find the place jammed. That's the way I envisioned this beach, as a place that must come alive after dark, when it would be crowded with people partying and gulls feasting.

The occasional patches of puréed seaweed that dotted the shoreline in Eastham and Wellfleet the day before were off Truro today in some force. Thick and unctuous, the dark mass bore a disturbing likeness to crude oil as sluggish waves eased it shoreward. A first-timer to the beach might well have found the sight shocking—it looked as if a sister of the *Exxon Valdez* had gone aground nearby. At that moment I said a quick prayer of thanks that oil and gas drilling on Georges Bank remains banned.

By early afternoon gulls started showing up (had they slept in, or gone on a run to the dump?), as did sanderlings and sandpipers. As usual, most of the gulls wandered about as aimlessly as beach bums, but two right at the water mark were engaged in some activity, and I went closer to look. Each had a hold on lunch, a fiddler crab in the wrong place at the wrong time, which the gulls were preparing to tear apart. At last: a Darwinian struggle in the flesh.

For a moment, the crab broke loose from the gulls. Waving the outsized claw frantically, he (the big claw is a male characteristic) seemed to be beckoning right at me in semaphore: "C'mere! C'mere! Help me! *Help* me!" The gesture seemed so human, I was on the verge of going to his rescue. But I came to my senses and refrained from shooing away the gulls. It was their lunch, after all, and reluctantly I let them have it. Anyway, what was I to do with the half-mangled fiddler?

This was "naked Nature" such as Thoreau confronted by the sea, "inhumanly sincere, wasting no thought on man, nibbling at the cliffy shore where gulls wheel amid the spray." And nibble on fiddler crabs. While I was being humanly insincere. Hadn't I slipped one of the crab's Maryland relatives—blue, buttered, and breaded—into a hot frying pan and thence down my own gullet just the other day?

I left the fiddler to his fate, but not without a small lump in my throat. While an eater of flesh and fowl, I'm also a confirmed anthropomorphist—I always get choked up when the antelope gets it on the PBS wildlife programs. I admit to finding "naked Nature" and the survival of the fittest in action somewhat disconcerting.

Ahead was another morsel-in-wait, a large surf clam (*Spisula solidissima*), the discarded shells of which live on in many cottages as ashtrays. During his travels H.T. once cooked a surf clam (to him a "hen-clam") over a fire and ate *the whole* thing (his emphasis) for his "nooning." With no intention of eating, just curious, I approached for an inspection, for this was the first intact surf clam I'd come across over many miles of beach walking. H.T. lost his lunch because of such a clam (a part of this variety should not be eaten); I nearly lost a finger. The clam's jaw was open a crack, and when I leaned down and poked it ever so slightly, it snapped shut in a flash. The quick response and sound of its powerful, sand-crunching jaw hinges sent me reeling back ten feet. It was beyond me how any denizen of this beach could tangle with such a clam and win, yet the beach was littered with the bleached skeletal remains of their many battlefield losses.

I suddenly became acutely aware of a peculiar odor, the likes of which I'd never inhaled before. It was not a familiar beach aroma, nothing like "good" low tide (with a hint of potassium and phosphate) or "bad" low tide (with a strong suggestion of sewage)—not at all piquant but short of being gaggingly noxious. Perhaps it had something to do with the heavy belt of seaweed, though most of it was not decomposing on the beach but remained just offshore. Whatever its source, the odor offered a stern challenge to the nostrils.

Along this stretch the beach not only smelled ripe but also was unkempt as a college dorm room. The culprit here was not man—there were no cups or beer cans—but "naked Nature" alone. Driftwood of every conceivable shape and size was scattered haphazardly across the sand, with sea wrack dumped helter-skelter to the high-water mark and well beyond. Not the least bit picturesque, it was still a most sublime shambles.

I was beginning to absorb some of H.T.'s beach lessons, gaining firsthand knowledge that nature is indifferent to our antiseptic sensibilities. Not quite pristine, not always pretty, at times savage and stinky, Truro's outer beach yet possesses a transcendent purity, a purity that could easily be overlooked by those who come here in search of beauty and order as humans define them.

The complexion of the beach was about to change once again. Ahead I saw vehicle tracks in the sand, so I knew I'd reached High Head. Recreational vehicles are not allowed on the National Seashore except for an eight-mile stretch from High Head to Hatches Harbor, Provincetown. It would be the first time during this walk that my solitude might be interrupted on a regular basis, for I was about to embark on a beach road that from all appearances was very well traveled.

III. High Head

I headed straight for off-road vehicle tracks, hoping the path might provide easier walking. No luck: the sand was just as deep and difficult to manage. I tried walking in the tire tracks, I tried the hump between the tracks, I tried the high-water mark, surf's edge, bank's edge — nothing offered any solid footing. Every now and then I'd hit some firmer ground, and so much energy would surge through me I felt as if I could walk around the earth at the Equator. But the good patches never lasted more than three footsteps. H.T. said of the Great Beach that "one mile there is as good as two elsewhere." This is true in the physical as well as the aesthetic sense, one mile in the heavy sand surely being equal to two on pavement.

Behind me an ORV approached, and I scrambled out of the way with a great deal of effort. The driver didn't acknowledge me, nor did a number of others who soon passed by, unlike pleasure boaters, who in their comradely spirit wave at everything from jet skis to ocean liners. Perhaps my appearance—barefoot in the middle of nowhere with notebook and camera in hand—pegged me as a radical environmentalist, of that ilk who have fought so hard to keep ORVs off the beach.

Actually, during my Cape years I often defended ORV use over the vociferous objections of my acquaintances. In the late 1980s the National Seashore had tried to defuse conflicts among various park-user groups by launching a public service campaign to "Share the Beach," and I'd come to embrace that philosophy. Now that I'd been out here at length I could confirm that the beach has plenty of room for everyone, and I saw no reason why recreational vehicles shouldn't continue to have *limited* access.

For years ORVs have been banned from large portions of the National Seashore for much the same reason cows were banned from the beach in the 1800s: their indiscriminate roaming had become a prime cause of erosion. The biggest controversy exploded a few years ago, when Seashore officials began to close off parts of *permitted* ORV routes during certain times of the year to protect the threatened piping plover, which, during nesting season, forages in the same part of the beach where Jeeps and pickups tread. The piping plover (*Charadrius melodus*), whose "dreary peep" made a deep impression on Thoreau, never gained the national notoriety of the snail darter or the spotted owl, but its plight unleashed a thousand passionate voices on Cape Cod.

Supporters of beach buggies mounted an aggressive campaign against the closings and, this being Old Cape Cod, spun some mighty good yarns in the process. Even people who had only recently moved to the outer Cape from New York talked about residents' "aboriginal rights" to unfettered beach access. One imaginative, oft-told, and no doubt apocryphal story pointing out the injustice of the buggy bans concerned an ancient surfcaster who supposedly had landed a huge striper and then collapsed with a coronary dragging the behemoth back to a distant parking lot. In this Yankee version of *The Old Man and the Sea,* the Jeepless surfcaster was the noble Santiago, while the feds, environmentalists, and the plover itself assumed the role of the greedy sharks who stripped the old man of his hard-earned catch.

After taking a public relations drubbing for their insistence in keeping ORV routes open during nesting season, the off-roaders later toned down their rhetoric. Their leaders learned that it doesn't pay to take on a cute feathery little thing whose advocates include those who buy ink by the barrel *and* the United States government.

The effort to increase plover numbers on the Cape continues. Ensuring the bird's protection from some humans has required a lot of intervention by other humans. Smart enough to feign injury and draw predators away from nests (a tactic H.T. witnessed), the plover also thinks that paper or plastic kites hovering overhead are hawks or other birds of prey waiting to pounce; it will remain motionless wherever it is if it spots a kite. Since this often leads to nests being left unattended in the hot sun, with hardboiled plover eggs the result, the Seashore also bans kite flying from the beach during nesting season.

Although I was walking down the middle of the main ORV lanes, traffic was extremely light, and most of the time the beach was as empty as ever. The gulls were with me, of course; the more they were with me the more my attitude toward them changed, and I soon began to look upon them favorably. They never once bothered me, and the anthropomorphist in me found it easy to fantasize that the birds' omnipresence was not coincidental but rather a sign of loyalty and devotion to the solitary barefoot walker. I would no longer begrudge them their fiddler crabs.

The plight of some gulls even earned my sympathy. There was one with a badly broken wing, no doubt a sentence to slow death. A few other birds stood alone; I could almost sense that they'd been ostracized, and they too looked like sad souls. What sort of offense do you suppose would earn a gull banishment from the flock?

In a place girded by sea and sand, baking under a hot sun, mirages and other visual tricks are occasional occurrences, and what I now espied on the beach ahead seemed designed to test my cognitive powers. I came upon the apparition suddenly, for whatever it was, it blended in well with the sand. It appeared to be a barefoot woman lying on the sand, and to my amazement I was right. Wearing a white haltertop, white jeans, and sunglasses, bearing a startling resemblance to the young Jackie Kennedy, she lay on her right side, bottom leg tucked under her, head on the sand facing seaward. She had no cooler, no blanket, no umbrella, no pocketbook. My surprise at running across this mystery figure was compounded by the improbable location, a good hike from any public areas. In covering nearly two-thirds of the National Seashore, I'd met no walkers beyond public beaches; this woman could have been left out here by dune buggy, but none had passed for some time.

She was alive; her chest rose and fell with her breathing and the big toe of her outstretched foot made constant circles in the sand. And her eyes were open behind the big oval sunglasses, I could tell. I thought of going over to speak with her.

But at second glance I saw that this was no Siren; if anything she was Garboesque, her body language fairly screaming that she wanted to be alone, that she was deeply disturbed. Whatever was upsetting her had likely driven her to this faraway lonely place to contemplate, to clear her head. I could appreciate that. And what if she didn't appreciate an intrusion?

I can deflect a put-down in a barroom, but just then one negative word or emotion could spell the ruination of an extraordinary day. Although my toes were bleeding, my legs ached, and even my glutes had started to protest, I'd fallen in step to a rhythm track laid down by nature, the beat carrying me to a plane hitherto unknown to me, a level where new sensations and experiences crowded out physical pain and other temporal concerns. I couldn't risk any interruption to this flow, so I walked on, leaving the reclining woman to her thoughts, and me to mine.

Hoping to get a fix on my location, I took a quick detour to the top of the sand ridge and looked in the direction of the parabolic dunes, a well-known sight to drivers entering Provincetown on Route 6. On the other side of dune country lay Pilgrim Lake and Provincetown, still hidden from view by the rolling sand and brush-covered hills. At some point around here Thoreau and Channing took a path to Provincetown (after doubling back from Race Point), but from this vantage point the dunes were a trackless wilderness, having no foot trails that I could discern. I decided to keep walking on to Race Point, and then to town, saving dune exploration for later.

Some distance had opened between me and the mystery woman when I had my first outer beach encounter with an ambulatory human, another woman. Carrying a pair of inappropriate shoes in her hand, she made me think that Race Point—the next closest public area—must be getting very near. This woman wanted to talk. She told me she was from Manhattan and staying in Provincetown for the weekend. She seemed underwhelmed by her surroundings and asked if there were any "grand views" to be seen out here.

"*Grand* views?" I asked, a bit perplexed.

"I mean, are there any lighthouses? Can you see the city and harbor from here, the big sailboats and such? Or is this *it*?"

I told her that Highland Light was miles away, too far for her to reach on foot, and that the view back to Provincetown (which had to be what she meant by "the city") was obscured, even from the heights of the sand bank. She appeared greatly let down, and I began to suspect that what she was searching for didn't exist, not here anyway. She'd walked a long way on hot sand, put America behind her, and was expecting something spectacular, a wonder of the world. Instead she'd found diffident gulls, dead skates swarming with beach fleas, and a surf gone flaccid under a heavy coat of mushy seaweed.

I understood her disappointment and didn't hold it against her. So many of us profess a longing to "get back to nature," but we expect to be blown away once we're there. Not used to solitude, we can become uncomfortable, even bored with it. There are indeed great discoveries waiting to be made on the outer beach, but it's no theme park. "It is even a trivial place," H.T. commented.

I became eager to get going, as my comrade from New York seemed content to linger and chat the afternoon away. "Maybe we'll see each other tonight in Provincetown and exchange stories," I said as I stepped away, being totally, humanly insincere.

She headed in the direction of High Head and I intended to move on, but I didn't. I stayed rooted right where I was, mulling over our conversation, thinking that perhaps I was racing *too* rapidly in the direction of my finish line at Race Point.

Out here where Truro meets Provincetown, where wrist connects with fist, the peninsula demonstrates quite a flex, and the walker is always rounding a point, constantly turning a corner. The hooking beach itself seems to conspire with the restless heart, its form feeding an irresistible urge to keep going, to look forward, to pursue the "grand view" that might loom beyond the next bend, impulses that make it tempting to bypass what's right at hand, and right at foot. I decided to resist those impulses and climbed to the top of the dune once more.

I sat down in a natural easy chair formed on the dune front, praying that I'd be able to get up again. The main attractions here were botanical, and for the first time I took notice of the beach plants, not to be confused with bayberry and other secondary dune plants, but rather those specimens that grow directly on the beach or in front of the sand and earthen bank.

At the foot of the dune where I lounged were some tufts of poverty grass, not half as lush as the variety growing back of the dunes; a half-buried sandwort, its stiff, stubby green fingers poking through the sand like a mummy's hand reaching out from the grave; and ground-creeping seaside spurge, spread and flattened on the beach fringe like a large squashed spider. In the immediate vicinity of my sandy seat I saw lots of Dusty Miller, which I recognized from gardens at home, the patterns of the pale green leaves vaguely resembling snowflakes magnified under a microscope. Nearby, more clumps of Dusty Miller orbited a single, stately tall wormwood, its willowy scrolled shoots displaying a dainty filigree that would make a master artisan envious.

The beach plants were easily overlooked; like roadside weeds, they straggle unassumingly along the entire stretch of sandy highway. The comparison to weeds is not inaccurate, but upon closer examination the lowly beach plants proved worthy of attention, and without fanfare they won my belated admiration. With the exception of Dusty Miller and tall wormwood, the plants are more homely than not, their most striking feature being their very existence in the beach's cruelest, most hostile neighborhood. Despite their proximity to the sea, beach plants cannot tolerate salt water, and their roots must dig deep into the earth to find fresh. Before getting up to go, I saluted their resilience and dogged will to survive.

I started back to the littoral zone, grateful that I'd taken a breather from the inexorable forward march to peruse some of the beach's less obvious pleasures. I was beginning to appreciate that the encompassing grandeur of the beach includes things mundane as well as sublime; there are indeed "grand views" to behold everywhere.

IV. Race Point

I was on a course west by north, bright sun almost dead ahead. The pesky seaweed was gone, the wind had freshened, and the sun's beam focused intently on an energized surf, walls of liquid emerald dissolving into foam so pure that ermine would look dingy next to it. It was the most dazzling white I'd ever seen, and by itself would have made the trip worthwhile—until now, I'd thought only Disney was capable of creating such gorgeous hues.

The sand embankment running along the beach was slowly dropping in elevation, the fifty-foot heights past Head of the Meadow reduced by about half. The beach here was steeper than at other spots, now becoming one smooth, upwardly slanting plane from water to dune. The frisky surf surged up the incline, straining to leave the beach behind, as if it had a hot date in P-town, and though its efforts appeared Sisyphean, some day it just might keep that date.

I'd gone without fluids since the Highland Golf Club— thinking to bring a water bottle was beyond my capacity—but I wasn't dying of thirst, despite the heat and exertion. Like H.T. I'd found that somehow the moist sea air helped to slake thirst.

Still, I was growing uncomfortably warm, and thought about taking a swim. Thoreau and Channing bathed in a pool between sandbars near Highland Light, but I'd seen no similar formations all along the outer beach; the recent series of tremendous storms obviously had wiped out a lot of bars, which tend to ameliorate rough conditions.

The chill water was not a deterrent, particularly with my adult layer of padding, but I was unable to gauge the lay of the shelf just offshore. Wary of currents and riptides, I decided not to risk even a quick dip. It was just as well. With my luck, I'd be caught with my shorts off when a ranger happened along (nudity is a Seashore no-no) or, if I kept my shorts on, I'd end up chafing all the way to Provincetown. Swimming was forgotten altogether when ahead I spotted the self-contained ORV campground. People look askance at solo swimmers in these waters, and I didn't want the campers to think a crazy man was wandering about their caravan.

This portion of the beach is set aside for motorized campers, and I saw a compact colony of recreational vehicles. Each unit appeared to come equipped with a standard complement of accessories, including a small "chase" vehicle (Jeep, generally) for making quick runs to town, and a type of skiff for open water fishing. A dozen radios blared baseball and football games, and many of the campers sported television antennas.

Despite trappings of affluence, the seaside trailer park had a down-home feel to it. For all their toys, for all the relative comfort in which they "roughed" it, I still got the sense that those who had set up housekeeping here would be at ease in the outdoors under any conditions. And while most were probably not on the Greenpeace mailing list, there were definite signs of respect and affection for this patch of wilderness. Noticeably, the area around the campsites was spotless, and every vehicle appeared to have a trash bag hung over the front fender gizmo that holds fishing rods. Some people may look down their noses at the mobile culture, but at least when these summer residents leave the Cape their seasonal homes go with them.

Along the shoreline dozens of fishing poles were set in the sand, some attended, some not. Lately I'd been hiking in the swash, which brought me directly underneath the lines. Not certain of the proper etiquette, I moved in a bit. Now I was in close contact with the inhabitants of the colony, most of whom paid me no attention. One woman, however, gave me a wide smile as she emerged from her trailer. I smiled back, wanting to ask her for a glass of water (not dying of thirst, I still had one) or better yet, a beer and a cigarette. I found it impossible to form any words, though—after a day of mostly solitary walking I'd become unbelievably bashful! She kept smiling, I kept smiling, and kept moving, feeling foolish but being unable to do anything about it.

With the exception of seaside goldenrod, like their landlubber namesake just now becoming profuse, reminders of the coming season were absent from the beach, which from all appearances remained in summer's thrall. Yet one hint of summer's end could be discerned in the ticking down of the world's oldest timepiece. By my reckoning it couldn't have been much past five o'clock, but the sun's rays had a distinct slant to them, and any object on the beach that could cast a shadow displayed one of a length that would cause the traveler to quicken the pace. Beston was right when he suggested that modern man has largely lost touch with the elemental world, but we've not yet evolved into total automatons. Modern society's obsession with time has kept us sensitive to its passage. I needed no watch to warn me to shake a leg.

Move I did, encouraged by signs of life ahead, which included dozens of kites skying high above the beach (plover nesting season was long over). There were lots of dogs, too, wearing bandannas, chasing Frisbees, and occasionally splashing into the surf, where no humans joined them. The New York woman passed by, heading back to Race Point sprawled out on the back of a pickup, a casualty of the beach. Her back was propped up against the cab and she had to twist her head to talk through the open glass partition with her rescuers.

With relief and no little bit of aching, I walked up the Race Point boardwalk (according to maps, this is Race Point *Beach*, Race Point itself being a little farther along). *Finis!* To my left was an old Life Saving Station, moved intact from Chatham and now serving as a museum; to my right, the old Race Point Coast Guard station, now the local National Seashore headquarters. Straight in front of me were the most wonderful landmarks of all: a public toilet and a water fountain.

I spent most of my toilet time looking in the mirror. I must say, I looked better than I felt, skin a healthy glowing reddish-brown, my thinning mane thickened and marcelled by the salt wind. I was ready for town.

I stopped for a drink at the fountain, where I took in enough to put a dent in the aquifer and send the waiting bicyclers behind me into near conniptions. Next, I walked over to the Seashore post. On the edge of a rise at Race Point Beach I was treated to a superlative view, similar to the one unfurled for H.T. at Highland, like that from the crow's nest of a ship at sea. In my mind's eye I could picture what lay beyond the horizon to the northwest, across the great divide of Massachusetts Bay: Cape Ann, the other great cape of the Commonwealth, Massachusetts' chunky left fist to Thoreau, "which keeps guard" on the state's breast while Cape Cod leads with a right, like John L. Sullivan sparring endless rounds with the oceanic heavyweight in their bare-knuckled fight to the finish.

As the sun slowly began to bow out of day, the arc of sea off Race Point became aluminum, looking like a foil-covered bowl, which reminded me: I was starving. Time to get to P-town and eat. Although it was not yet time, prevailing conditions suggested a perfect setup for a Homeric sundown such as the one H.T. and Channing watched from bayside Truro, when "the shining torch of the sun fell into the ocean." But even before I headed off, things changed. A billowing bank of clouds suddenly sprang up out of the horizon to squelch the show, and I could see there'd be no grand finale today. Instead, the sun unobtrusively slipped into a slit in the clouds, like a gold watch dropped into a vest pocket, and was gone.

It was off to Provincetown through the Provincelands. The sun had disappeared, but there was still some daylight left to guide me.

KARL B. WYCROFF

6

Provincetown

This was the most completely maritime

town that we were ever in.

CAPE COD

1. Labor Day Eve

There are two basic ways to get to Provincetown from Race Point: via the road or via the bike path through the Provincelands. I chose the latter, for I knew it would offer more interesting sights. The Provincelands have a roller coaster terrain, and I welcomed the paved bike paths. But even with my sneakers back on, it took me a while to establish a normal gait; after a day in soft sand my uncertain tread was not unlike that of a sailor who doesn't yet have his land legs.

A fair number of people were pedaling along the bike path. Almost invariably those coming down the hills were teens, speeding and showing off, while those heading up were families with little kids, many walking their bikes because of the grade. "Come on, Megan, keep up with us," one bearded dad shouted to his suffering daughter trailing behind, a little peanut holding on to her tiny three-speed with ebbing strength. Oh, these modern parents! Some of them think a proper family vacation has to be like boot camp. My father was not perfect by any means, but he was unmatched at showing us kids a good time on holiday at the beach — no straining or heavy lifting on old Dad's itinerary. I wondered what kind of Cape Cod memories exhausted little Megan would take home.

Despite the crowds of people biking back and forth, nothing could detract from the fact that the Provincelands are among the Cape's, if not the earth's, most forbidding stretches. God's mercy on the mariner who found himself shipwrecked upon this desolate wild in the days before Life Saving Stations and the coastal guards. The sand even has an ominous dark tinge to it, calling to mind what we as kids at the playground called "devil dirt," a layer of earth beyond the topsoil whose presence warned us we'd dug deep enough to reach the outskirts of Hell. The Provincelands have been in the public domain throughout history, and no wonder: who'd want to take title to this spooky acreage?

In other parts of the Provincetown Spit, sand moves relentlessly inland in the form of big waves, but in the Provincelands the march is more insidious, with sand seeping forward like a slowly rising tide, filtering around this tree, then that one, eventually strangling the life out of all in its path. The overall effect is similar to that of a World War I battlefield, a no man's land, the stunted, sandblasted, desiccated pines and oaks taking on grotesque shapes in death.

What does grow here grows desperately. The living pitch pines can hardly be called trees. They're little more than ground cover, and they glow with an eerie, almost unnatural neon green. The healthy verdant beach grass of other locales is here sickly yellow, spindly, sparse. Pale green lichens, however, plants of the tundra, find the Provincelands a compatible place.

From this stark country I walked into the deep cool of an arbor. It was a shocking change. Average-sized trees, so unexpected in this bleak place, blocked out not only the day's remaining light but also the noise of the distant beach and bike paths. It was so dark, so hushed, I almost genuflected. Quickly I realized I was in the much touted beech forest. According to the guidebook, it was 1.9 miles from beach to beech.

The "forest" is not much more than a modest grove, but its very existence here prompted me to ponder a topic of debate that every student of Cape Cod history inevitably confronts: how forested was it?

It's generally agreed today that much of the Cape was well-wooded when Europeans first arrived. Floors and other planking from old Cape houses offer proof that native trees at one time reached substantial size. But over the centuries settlers stripped the Cape's woodlands bare, first to open up land for farming and later to make products for every utility imaginable, from shipbuilding and other marine trades to the wood-burning glass, salt, and whale-trying works. (The widespread pitch pine plantations, whose success is so evident today, were undertaken as last-ditch remedies to the earlier destruction.)

Experts still don't agree, though, to what an extent forest covered the tract of land's end where I now walked. When the Pilgrims first rounded the Cape's tip, their chronicler reported it to be "all wooded with oaks, pines, sassafras, juniper, birch, holly, vines, some ash, walnut." Two hundred twenty-nine years later, H.T. gently chided the Pilgrims' observations, which he chalked up to their having been too long at sea: "I cannot but think that we must make some allowance for the greenness of the Pilgrims in these matters, which caused them to see green. We do not believe that the trees were large or the soil was deep here." One hundred forty years after Thoreau, the writer Cynthia Huntington wrote of this postglacial sand spit: "When the ocean makes land it creates something different from land's land. No bedrock, or heavy humus and clay, no hard-packed soil to clasp the roots of big trees and fold records of time in its layers."

Leave it to philosophers and poets to straighten out the Pilgrims. My own instincts tell me that Thoreau and Huntington are correct in doubting the existence of a great forest at the tip of the Cape. In other parts of New England, old cut forests have grown back tall and strong; if there was once an impressive wood here, why has it not also seen a revival? Back in Boston there are beech trees with trunks as imposing as the legs of wooly mammoths that roamed this land before the glaciers; the beech trees here, however, are almost wispy, and they don't appear particularly healthy.

Bennet Pond, thick with lily pads, was another unexpected find. Though Race Point was now two miles behind, the beach environment had seared itself into my consciousness, and it took some getting used to an "inland" landscape again. Past the pond was a fork in the path, and some signage I found confusing. Some cyclers went by me and nodded, but I refrained from asking them directions to town. Some people call the inability to acknowledge being lost a classic "guy thing," but I prefer to look at it as a demonstration of Emersonian self-reliance. As it turned out, my reliance was poorly placed—the fork I chose led to a dead end in thick woods, a futile twenty-minute diversion that tested the limits of my endurance. I could feel a dampness in my socks: my toes were bleeding again.

At last I emerged from the forest and reached Race Point Road.

I knew I'd finally got one turn right when I passed the town dump. Ahead was the Pilgrim Monument, its tower outlined against the deepening sky like an exclamation point — *Provincetown!*

The beach route to Race Point had brought me to a point well above and beyond the "Entering Provincetown" sign. This, then, was the side entrance to town, which led me across Route 6 to Conwell Street to Cemetery Road to Bradford Street, one of Provincetown's two major parallel thoroughfares. Commercial Street, the waterfront-hugging lane well known to H.T., was now just a block over.

Bradford was strangely quiet, practically deserted, reminding me of a sci-fi movie in which the streets have been cleared by reports of a Martian invasion. I crossed it and continued on Standish, looking straight down to MacMillan Wharf. Just as when I had stumbled into the beech forest, I was unprepared for the radical change in scenery that greeted me at the intersection of Standish and Commercial, Provincetown's version of Times Square. Commercial Street was alive with people, teeming with them, hundreds upon hundreds packed into the narrow old cart path. *There* was everyone. In Provincetown, H.T. remarked, "you are pretty sure to meet all the inhabitants who come out in the course of a day." I seemed to have met them all at once, and stood for a moment gawking, unsure, like a hick come to the big city for the first time.

There are lots of coastal towns in the United States, but far fewer are the enclaves that exist well beyond the continent's confines. Provincetown stands out among the latter as one of geography's *ne plus ultras.* (Key West, which is Provincetown with palm trees, is another.) At land's end, road's end, Provincetown is the outermost town, a freewheeling hamlet on the eastern frontier, where something of a frontier ethos still holds sway.

Full of art galleries and other venues of culture, Provincetown has no inhibitions about showing off its cheeky and cheesy sides as well. Here tacky T-shirt emporia jostle for space with hand-tooled leather and jewelry shops. And although the town lays claim to being gastronomically sophisticated, the first smell I distinguished was that unambiguously American aroma indigenous to every midway, every boardwalk from Presque Isle to Point Loma: that unmistakable honky-tonk mélange of pizza, popcorn, hot dogs, and beef tallow crackling in fired-up deep-fat fryers. Fittingly, Commercial Street this twilight was suffused with the soft butterscotch glow of carnival light.

Thoreau found in 1849 a Provincetown that "apparently is what is called a flourishing town," an important Massachusetts seaport of twenty-six hundred people. A huge mackerel fleet had just dropped anchor, and H.T., Channing, and the fishermen had to take turns flattening themselves against storefronts to make room for all the people to pass. I had no such option; I was immediately swept up and pushed west, which fortunately was in the direction I wanted to go. The flow of people had a palpable energy, which sucked me up and carried me along like an ocean beach undertow. I was on the right side of the street, with an eastbound stream to my left, so at least rudimentary rules of the road were observed.

According to the local Chamber of Commerce brochure, those partaking in Provincetown's summer-long bacchanalia comprise "at least two of everything. Tall. Short. Fat. Slim. Dressy. Simple. Gay. Straight."

It would be just like the relatively conservative Chamber to try to slip that one right by, relegating sexual orientation to the bottom rungs of its hierarchy. The fact is, more than tall people or dressy people or even a strong Portuguese community, homosexuals—both year-rounders and summer visitors—make up the dominant culture here today, the numbers, influence, and style of the gay community helping define Provincetown to a degree that no other group can approach. Indeed, the expression "One in Ten" could refer to the number of straights in town on certain summer days, when Provincetown is among the gayest places in the world.

There's no doubt how H.T. would regard modern Provincetown's tendencies toward intemperance and crass materialism, but how would he react to the town's ascendant culture? A number of gay scholars have in fact claimed Thoreau as one of their own. His work has been published in gay literary anthologies, and some have worked diligently to "out" him, looking to add Thoreau to the pantheon of great historical homosexuals. Professor Walter Harding, a noted Thoreau scholar, has concluded that H.T.'s "affectional orientation" was probably homosexual. Even Harding's, though, is at best an educated guess; it's likely that H.T. died a virgin.

Exercises in modern psychobiography get tiresome fast, and it seems rather pointless to talk about the hypothetical sexual preferences of a lifelong celibate. But just to balance the account, it should be pointed out that as a young man Thoreau was smitten with and courted a woman named Ellen Sewall, who eventually spurned both H.T. and his brother John to marry another. It's been suggested that, having lost the great love of his life, H.T. thereafter focused his affection and attention on the body of his life's work, moving in circles that were largely but not exclusively male. On his deathbed, where you expect the truth to be told, Thoreau said of Ellen, "I have always loved her."

The human tide swept me to the Seamen's Bank, where I took out a little cash, then back to the center of town. I was hungry, I was thirsty, I was tired, and here I was in a packed Cape town just after 7 P.M. on the last official weekend of summer, with conga lines snaking out the entrance to every single restaurant. I am differently timed, I thought.

With unbelievable luck, I found an immediate opening in a restaurant on Bradford Street. My small table was under the eaves in a darkened room, with a candle for atmospheric lighting. H.T. might have dined like this, except that his meal choices would have been severely limited. Poor Thoreau and Channing—every Provincetown restaurant offered the hungry pilgrims only two less-than-mouth-watering alternatives: hashed beans or hashed fish. Imagine:

"Good evening. Call me Ishmael; I'll be your waiter. May I get you some intoxicating liquids from the bar? No? Then let me tell you tonight's and every night's specials: hashed beans or hashed fish. Don't even think of asking for fresh fish—this is 1849, we don't *do* fresh fish in Provincetown—and *no* substitutions."

Even the Spartan-living Thoreau was a bit dismayed by the set menu. He probably had his heart set on a nice piece of broiled scrod. He opted for the beans, "though they were never a favorite dish of mine," having witnessed firsthand the unsanitary conditions under which codfish were cured on the Provincetown wharves, where, he punned, onlookers "were cured of eating them."

Provincetown today prides itself on its fine cuisine. It's not on a par with Boston's best, though, and I can say that I've never had a truly memorable meal there. My choices this night included the following specials, recited by the bartender, who doubled as my waitress: tournedos of beef with scallion and mushroom sauce, $21; salmon-stuffed ravioli, $22; and the chef's choice, oriental marinated tuna, served rare unless otherwise specified, $21. The last item made me smile. Joseph Lincoln, a popular Cape writer of the early twentieth century, tells how the old-timers despised tuna because the powerful fish would rip the nets when they became caught in fixed weirs. After clubbing tuna—which they derisively dubbed "horse mackerel"—to death, trap fishermen would leave them to rot on the beach. Now, not only does a slice of this horse mackerel command a double-sawbuck tariff in restaurants, but Japanese buyers bid top dollar on MacMillan for whole tuna, which are then air-freighted directly to Tokyo sushi bars.

I love fish, but something about the price of *frutos do mar* in Provincetown brought out the frugal Yankee in me, and so I ordered a chicken dish, the closest thing they had to hashed beans.

The lounge was filling up with people waiting for tables downstairs. It was an almost entirely gay gathering, with everyone seemingly in a feverish, end-of-summer mood, anxious as it was jovial. There was a lot of touching going on, the body language aggressive and possessive, staking claim for the final fling. It occurred to me that I might be the only person in all of Provincetown dining solo this evening. I didn't mind; while on the whole preferring good company and conversation, being inclined to sip solitude rather than drink it deeply as Thoreau did, I'm not afraid to be alone and have grown used to entertaining myself.

Even though Provincetown was hopping, my poor old legs were achy and throbbing. Although I'm in reasonably good physical condition, walking from Highland Light to Provincetown via the beach on a hot summer day had been without a doubt the toughest physical challenge I'd ever undertaken. With mission and dinner completed I was euphoric, but not enough to ignore my imminent collapse. The only boogeying I did was down to the Chamber of Commerce office, to grab a cab back to base camp. Rest assured that I intended to retrace on foot every inch taken by car.

Unlike Wellfleet, Provincetown is a taxi town. My driver was a barrel-chested guy in his late fifties or early sixties, straight out of central casting. After I told him where I was headed, he immediately launched into a spontaneous monologue. "I'm native Provincetown," he informed me earnestly. "Portagee. Family's been here over a hundred years." To me, his ethnicity was quite obvious, despite his Anglicized name. Herman Wouk has written that Russians so resemble one another they appear to be a nation of first cousins, and I would argue that the same holds true for the Portuguese. My driver looked exactly like the cop directing traffic in front of Town Hall, who was the twin of a guy dishing out fried clams and soft-serve ice cream by the Chamber of Commerce, whose *doppelgänger* even now was repairing fishing nets on MacMillan.

I knew what was coming next when, during a rare pause in his autobiography, I was able to ask the driver how business was. "Terrible, just terrible, the worst year I can remember." And I've heard this same plaint every year I can remember since first coming to the Cape. Mind you, this was a town where every inn had a "No Vacancy" sign posted out front, where the wait for a table was two hours, minimum. I've always suspected that the locals think anyone asking questions about their business must be undercover IRS agents.

I put my head back on the seat and might have even started to doze off, but when the driver started talking about Norman Mailer, a fairly well-known seasonal P-town resident, I snapped to attention. It was a tortuous tale involving, as I recollect, Mailer, an unpaid bar tab, a brawl, the Provincetown police, and the subsequent "unjust" canning of an arresting officer.

"That's quite a story," I told the driver. "And when did all this happen?"

"Let's see. 1958."

1958? Was that his most up-to-date Mailer yarn? Don't tell me Norman's been on good behavior for almost forty years!

We were at the motel parking lot. I paid the *prix fixe* fare and added a large tip, which the driver must have felt he hadn't worked hard enough for, since he started in on a new round of P-town celebrity gossip. When he commenced to talk about "young" Marlon Brando I cut him off, telling him it was past my bedtime, and thanking him for the educational ride.

Before bed, I stopped in for a nightcap at Goody Hallett's, which was more crowded than the previous night, but still nowhere near capacity. My Wellfleet oystermen were not in residence, and when I asked if anyone had seen them, I was met with shrugs and blank stares. I sidled up to a stool next to two women and ordered a drink.

After my day of solitude, all of a sudden I felt like a dam near ready to burst with torrents of garrulity. I wanted to tell them about a journey that began from this exact point half a day ago, a story of pluck and determination and lacerated toes, replete with observations into the nature of gulls, fiddler crabs, natural selection, and the survival of the fittest—and complete with allusions to our famous New England forebear, Henry David Thoreau.

I offered to buy the women a drink, but they politely refused. "The society of young women is the most unprofitable I have ever tried," H.T. once wrote, and for once I had to agree. I returned to my room and spent the time before retiring in a more profitable manner, washing out my bloodstained socks in the motel room sink.

II. Monday, Labor Day

In the morning, not very hungry, I headed down the road that would take me back to Provincetown to catch the Boston ferry, as was H.T.'s custom when leaving the Cape.

I stopped for a cup of coffee and headed along 6A, a somnolent stretch of road that the Cape's boom times have so far largely bypassed. Five minutes from the *Hound of the Baskervilles* setting of the Highland moors, 6A could be a country lane in any American town, with intermittent homesteads punctuated by small groves of trees and fields of impenetrable bramble, of the variety that tore the Pilgrims' armor when they tramped through this neighborhood in 1620.

About Truro, Gertrude Stein would never have said, "There's no there there," as she had about Oakland, but it can be said in a variation on her theme that in the Town of Truro, there is no town of Truro. It has no central locus; it's more or less a loose association of far-flung neighborhoods, none of which attains true village status. There's something of the tongue-in-cheek about a sign on Route 6 directing travelers to "Downtown Truro," for it leads only to a tiny mall along the Pamet River. If the police station and town offices were next door, "Downtown Truro" would be a proper village, but those buildings are down the road a piece.

Quiet prevailed along 6A; not a soul was about, not even at a couple of cottage colonies advertising "No Vacancy." When H.T. visited Truro, the town (indeed, the Cape) was largely devoid of a male presence; most of the menfolk were before the mast. It appeared to Thoreau "as if every able-bodied man and helpful boy in the Bay had gone out on a pleasure excursion on their yachts, and all would at last land and have a chowder on the Cape." The rather idyllic imagery he must have meant to be ironic, for as H.T. was well aware, there was little pleasure to be found in an occupation that tallied fifty-seven Truro residents lost in "the memorable gale of 1841" alone.

Today there looked to be a small fishing or lobster boat dry-docked in every other driveway. Like ghost ships, the untended "yachts" showed no signs of life, and the neighborhood was as still as it might have been in 1849. Having at last landed, were skippers and crew now busy at their chowder? I had no idea why all these boats were reduced to floating on gravel and tar—it might have been some seasonal thing—but to me they stood out as sad symbols of a fishing industry gone to rot.

A few minutes later I came upon a possible clue as to the whereabouts of Truro's beached fishermen and weekend cottage dwellers: two small restaurants were doing land-office business for breakfast. The smells were tempting, but I would pass up breakfast and take my nooning in Provincetown, where I could keep a close eye on the 3:30 ferry.

At a crest in the road, Truro's knobby hills and furtive hollows gave way in an eyeblink to a wide-angled shot of the Cape's outer limits, the peninsula at its terminus nearly doubled over "like a cod in a pot," to filch a phrase from Joyce. It was a busy picture, the view taking in an unbroken line of bay-fronting motels and cottages dead ahead, with populous Provincetown at a diagonal across the water a few miles distant.

In addition to the Pilgrim Monument and two water towers of robin's egg blue, Provincetown's skyline is graced by other landmarks, and with an assist from memory I could distinguish three of them through thin haze: from west to east, the Universalist Church (1847), Town Hall (1886), and the Heritage Museum (1860), formerly the Methodist Church.* As I admired the town's impressive profile, it struck me that the whaling and Grand Banks captains designed their churches and civic center to be like their ships, strong, solid, able to withstand adversity, built to last. The steeples of Provincetown have heft, the big spires jutting confidently toward the heavens, more than ready to take whatever the North Atlantic dishes out.

I slipped onto the bay beach through an opening between motels. What a change from the Great Beach! A docile surf barely roamed from its breaking point, and the walking, sneakered or barefoot, was a breeze. Thoreau wrote that the bay beach "was harder than on the Backside," and I likewise found the terra here definitely firma, as a Bostonian might put it.

As noontime approached, both bay and sky were in the mildest of moods, the wan sun generally content to laze behind a high, thin layer of clouds. Once in a while El Sol deigned to show its entire face, warming the day and silvering the bay, which fluttered lightly in the gentle breeze, a sun spangled banner. About fifty yards off the beach, a becalmed windsurfer shunted his sail about in a herculean effort to catch an elusive edge of wind. Farther offshore a large schooner in full sail had managed to escape the doldrums and was knifing around Long Point, where the Cape tapers off into Provincetown Harbor, the great peninsula concluding as a simple sandbar a child could straddle. (The vessel, I would learn later, was the gaff-rigged schooner *Bay Lady II*, available for pleasure cruising from MacMillan Wharf.)

*The Methodists later built a church more suitable to their needs on Shank Painter Road.

These few select images—sailing vessel, sequined bay, Long Point and its lighthouse—offered tantalizing hints as to how the harbor must have looked in 1849, when H.T. observed two hundred boats of the mackerel fleet putting in at Provincetown. If the sight of a single vessel under sail can stir the modern soul so, imagine the grandeur of such a scene multiplied two hundred times! It's no mystery why the Tall Ships pageants have proved so popular.

Gazing seaward made me wax nostalgic about glory days of a golden age under sail, and yet I was also aware that this very beach had known gory days as well. In July 1855 Thoreau stood here and watched pilot whales being herded ashore and slaughtered for their oil, a bloody episode he recounted in *Cape Cod* with lively style but little editorial comment. ("Save the Whales" sentiments were still a century away from coming into vogue.) While the kill was important to the livelihoods of local subsistence fishermen, the hunting of whales, whether by large fleets at sea or small inshore posses, is one bygone Cape tradition we don't wish to memorialize. (Nowadays when pilot whales beach themselves for reasons unknown, a Capewide whale rescue network springs into action. More rugged volunteers even go to sea to help free endangered right whales from the entanglements of fishing and lobster lines.)

I passed a long row of small waterfront cottages familiar to those who know the work of photographer Joel Meyerowitz, two dozen identical white clapboard structures with green trim and gabled roofs, set shoulder to shoulder on the beach like so many cabanas. Not so much as a scrap of paper disrupted the perfection of the scene. Was it pride of tenancy?

Leaving the sandy yards of the cabana cottages behind, I returned to Route 6A, walking past front entrances of larger bay-front cottages bearing names like Tijoda, Salt Spray, and Maushop's Rest. At this narrow point of the Cape, Route 6A is only yards away from Route 6, the one fronting the bay, the other edging Pilgrim Lake, with the dunes and the Atlantic beyond. Pilgrim Lake is the landlocked remnant of East Harbor, which used to open up onto the bay. Tijoda, Salt Spray, and Maushop's Rest—all the cottages sit on a built-up barrier beach of fairly recent origin, while the two roads are in effect causeways. Because East Harbor/Pilgrim Lake was still open water at the time of H.T.'s visits, he had to go through dune country and come into Provincetown from the ocean side.

At the entrance to Provincetown, Commercial Street and the East End, our paths—H.T.'s and mine—rejoined. On his first visit, the street was made up of four planks set down over sand. On the water side, he wrote, were the fish and storehouses, while on the inner side stood houses "in which a more modern and pretending style has at length prevailed over the fisherman's hut."

Vestiges of this arrangement are readily apparent. Now desirable if still largely unpretentious, renovated waterfront quarters, laid out in a jumble of shapes and sizes, remain redolent of their shanty past. Today the bleached-shingle styling is livened by splashes of color, with shutters and doors showing bright trim, and flowers everywhere, spilling out of window boxes, bordering shell or brick walkways, crowding tiny plots of front yard.

Half a dozen paces across the road, the "more modern and pretending" homes on the inner side of Commercial Street's east end show a variety of architectural styles, one after the other: Greek Revival, Second Empire, Federalist, and so on. The inner side, east-end homes were obviously built and first occupied by the town nobs (who I'm quite sure never kvetched about the neighboring fish shanties "spoiling the view"), and both the houses and their grounds are more substantial than I remembered from days when I used to pass through here in a news van on tight deadline. A few more paces and I quickly realized that a walk along the streets affords a far more detailed look at Provincetown's layout than you can get from the claustrophobic vantage point of an automobile, even one slowly creeping. For the first time I was able to observe up close that while Provincetown is "tightly compacted" it is not necessarily built all wall-to-wall.

During H.T.'s stopover, one Provincetown resident told him that "it was the custom there to be abed very late on Sunday, it being a day of rest." On this Monday holiday the streets had a quiet, old-fashioned Sabbath feel. The mood started to change as I continued west on Commercial, and there was a general stirring on the approaches to the town's center. As I walked I looked for the site of the Pilgrim House, a hotel at which H.T. had stayed, destroyed by fire sometime in the late 1980s. I poked my head into a little alleyway adjacent to the Pilgrim House art gallery and, as if reading my mind, a man with a gray ponytail came out of a storefront. "You looking for the original Pilgrim House? It was back there, where the shops are. Somebody put too many shrimp on the barby one night and *it burned down!*" He laughed heartily at his own witticism. That was a good one—arson was suspected, as I recall, and I'm quite sure overcooked shrimp had nothing to do with it.

By the time I reached Town Hall, Provincetown was fully awake and, always surprising in a place surrounded by the sea, oppressively hot. The Boston ferry, the *Provincetown II*, was in for its three-hour layover, adding a couple hundred more day-trippers to the growing mob. Because I've taken the boat on many occasions, I knew that some of the passengers don't wander far from the ferry to assure themselves of an inside seat with a table for the ride home. More adventurous passengers fan out to restaurants and shops, with not a few heading directly for the benches in front of Town Hall, a prime location for gawking. Like most resorts, Provincetown can be a real rip-off, but the show on Commercial Street is free and well worth the trip. This is major league people watching. Eye browsing is expected, even encouraged; according to one local guide, the famous Spiritus Pizza shop near Town Hall is also known as "Stare-at-Us." The audience is happy to oblige, looking not with sidelong glances or the cursory once-over one might give the passing parade at, say, Quincy Market or the local mall, but rather with open gazes of undisguised curiosity.

Everyone knows that everyone else is sizing them up, and why (no, it's not to ascertain if they're tall, short, fat, slim, dressy, simple), and the fishbowl syndrome in turn informs pedestrian behavior. Those under scrutiny, whether willing participants in the Provincetown Promenade or just passersby, seem quite adamant that the peanut gallery not peg them wrongly, and as a result, Provincetown is the most demonstrative place I've ever been in. There's an inordinate amount (for broad daylight) of proprietary hand holding and tight hugging, to the extent you'd think the town was hosting a convention of Siamese twins, all joined at the hip and shoulders. Straight couples especially cling to each other fiercely, as if to eliminate any possible ambiguity.

I headed back to the waterfront for my nooning, determined to keep an eye on the ferry, as some fear about missing it kept nagging at me. I couldn't miss it, as I had to be at work in the morning, and also because after today the ferry would run only on weekends.

The outdoor deck of the Surf Club at the foot of MacMillan Wharf offered the perfect site for ferry watching. Although I had a hankering for a plate of greasy fried clams, the restaurant was out of bellies, and the Mulloneys do not eat clam strips. My server was a tall, dignified man of impeccable bearing who looked out of place among this harried, hurried boat crowd. He looked so competent that when he recommended the fish sandwich, I couldn't pass it up.

With a fishing boat beached right in front of the restaurant, its frayed nets strung out across the grimy sand, and the rest of the colorful fleet with the colorful names tied up just beyond, on MacMillan's lee side, the scene looked much as it must have at the turn of the century, when Provincetown's Mediterranean flavor first attracted renowned artists to its bustling waterfront. But to sketch a realistic picture of Provincetown's fishing industry today would be to draw a veritable still life, and when the waiter brought my sandwich, a huge slab of some kind of white fish, I was quite sure it wasn't landed by a boat out of this harbor.

The port and its small aging day boats have been in a long, slow decline, victims of circumstance for the most part, now paying a price for the voracious appetites of bigger boats from bigger harbors. Today there was only one refrigerated truck on the wharf to take the catch to market, nothing on the magnitude of New Bedford or Gloucester, themselves reeling from overfishing and the industry's near-total collapse. (Tuna fishing could be considered one possible exception to Provincetown's fading fortunes, but that seasonal pursuit is at best hit or miss.) Some years back I had interviewed a local fisherman, who told me he'd just purchased a vintage seventy-two-foot eastern stern trawler. When I asked if he was expanding his fleet with an eye to better days ahead, he had laughed and said: "No, no, I'm planning to fix her up and turn her into a floating museum to preserve the story of P-town's fishing heritage. That's the only future that baby's got."

Provincetown's present maritime success story is berthed on

the side of MacMillan opposite the tired fishing boats in the form of sleek modern vessels of the whale-watching fleet, many operated by sons and daughters of old seafaring families who've been able to adapt to the times. But while whale watching can be a lucrative business, there's little connected to making a living from the sea that's a sure thing; the whales, though intelligent creatures, remain oblivious to their important role in Provincetown's economy and are reported to be finding better summer feeding grounds in areas that could eventually take this whale-watching fleet out of the loop.

Boasting an exceptional harbor and a plethora of amenities within hailing distance of the docks, Provincetown oddly enough does not attract pleasure boats in any significant numbers. There have been proposals to develop first-class marinas as a way to keep the harbor vibrant, but in typical P-town fashion this topic tends to divide the locals. One debate flash point has always been the "character" issue: that is, what impact might marinas and yacht clubs have on P-town's funky ambiance? One word I've heard spoken around here with fear and loathing is *Nantucket*.

Perhaps Nantucket did change with an infusion of big money, but I think local fears about the monogram set's establishing an anchorage here are unfounded; it could never be the right fit. Homophobia is part of it; also, this is a populist town to the bone, inclusive rather than exclusive, and it protects its (plebeian) pedigree as fiercely as any Back Bay blue blood protects his. Foolish as it may seem, that Chamber of Commerce guide speaks the truth—Provincetown *is* a place with at least two of everything; it's *déclassé* as it is chic, equally popular with transvestites and blue-haired grannies (who cannot always be easily told apart). But P-town and yachts? I don't think so.

✣

Boarding for the trip to Boston began on the *Provincetown II*, and I took a seat on deck to watch stragglers sprint down the wharf. There were lots of tearful bon voyages; some of the leavetakings seemed overwrought, considering that we were about to journey all of fifty-five nautical miles. Then it registered again: Provincetown to Boston is more than twice the distance that separates England from France. (There are no boats after Columbus Day, and no Chunnel here.) The tears might have belonged to Year-Rounders (proud of the appellation, Provincetowners capitalize it) and visitors who had struck up summer romances, not to be reunited with lovers until next season, if ever.

Dockside, one woman in a smart black top, gold lamé skirt, and mink stole was on the verge of hysteria, caterwauling and wiping her eyes. Next to me, a boy of about eight spotted the distressing scene and yelled at the top of his lungs, "Hey, who're you? Mom, who's that guy all dressed up?" The entire boat heard him, and everyone cracked up.

Out of the mouths of babes. I recognized the transvestite as a performer in town; I'd seen his picture in the entertainment guide back at my motel. He put on a good show here and helped lift the mood of a mostly unhappy-looking boatload of people. But like those holding "bridge" parties this very moment along Route 6 on the Upper Cape, where locals hang bedsheets reading "See you next year" at overpasses in view of departing traffic, our weeper's Labor Day gesture of Godspeed was mainly symbolic. The season wasn't over yet by a long shot; the boatloads and carloads would keep coming. And I'd be among them.

The *Provincetown II* backed out of its berth under the watchful eyes of dozens of cormorants on the breakwater and was rounding Long Point within moments. Shortly thereafter I was fishing through my backpack for a sweater. Still in sight of steamy Provincetown, we were now "about to float over melting icebergs," as H.T. described the predictable climatic change whose numbing effect he too had felt on his Provincetown-Boston excursions.

There had been a cover of high clouds all day, but as we plowed on to Boston across the bay, the sky took on a puckered look, known to mariners as the mackerel sky: a front was heading right for us, bringing with it rain.

On open water the movement's metamorphoses were easy to follow. The mackerel sky quickly thickened like a pan of *roux* on a hot stove, a witch's *roux*, dark and malevolent-looking; then, as if a clumsy hand on high had upset the pan, the inky mass began slowly seeping west to east. Next, up popped small puffs of curdling clouds, white as steam, innocuous looking in themselves, but quite ominous superimposed on the lowering sky. With everything in place, the heavens proceeded to open.

It was a textbook display of a storm's formation, and with the rains the lesson ended, driving most on the exposed decks indoors. Some joined in line dancing to a Dixieland band, and some went to the bar. Others, green around the gills, headed for this deck's benches, which run the length of the ship on both port and starboard sides, where they joined those already stretched out. While some parts of the *Provincetown II* were growing jolly, others looked like a hospital ship. This onboard outbreak of agonized gizzards had to be the result of dissipation, for the storm had brought with it not a breath of wind, and the only marks on an otherwise satiny sea were electric pulses of energy pushed out by the probing bow of the smooth-sailing ferryboat.

The ship was running through a gauntlet of lobster trap buoys that, as it turned out, stretched clear across Massachusetts Bay almost from Provincetown Harbor right into Boston Harbor.

Soon ahead off the port bow I could make out Minot Light. Minot was designed to warn ships away from the treacherous rock ledges that extend from the Cohasset and Scituate shoreline; it is itself anchored to a ledge, no island or house surrounding, only open water, so that the lighthouse appears to be emerging from the depths, like a Polaris missile launched from a submarine lurking below.

During Thoreau's 1849 voyage back to Boston, the Minot lighthouse then under construction was in the shape of an egg, and mounted on iron pillars. Thoreau wondered what it would be like to tend such a place: "Think of making your bed thus in the crest of a breaker! To have the waves, like a pack of hungry wolves, eyeing you always, night and day, and from time to time making a spring at you, almost sure to have you at last." That superb passage, which I recalled as we glided past the contemporary mechanized lighthouse, gave me shivers: an 1851 storm had swept the egg-shaped lighthouse, along with its two keepers, into oblivion.

Soon we approached the spread of rockbound Outer Harbor islands, their lighthouses glinting like diamond rings on a wiseguy's knuckles. It started to clear in the distant west, which brought the skyline of Boston into vague view, the Prudential Building and "new" Hancock Tower standing aloof and imperious southwest of downtown, the rest of the skyscrapers clustered around the waterfront and the Financial District. A number of the latter structures have distinctive shapes, but darkened for the holiday and now backlit by a late-emerging sun, the skyline's silhouette took on a generic, cardboard cutout look, like a graphic designer's poster: *The City*.

The City appeared to be dead, but its massive public works projects were alive, even on this day set aside to honor working folk. Dredging for the third harbor tunnel was going on almost dead ahead in the narrowing channel, and sparks of welding could be seen coming from the Deer Island Sewage Treatment Plant to starboard.

The Deer Island project is part of an industrial effort of mammoth proportions aimed at cleaning up a harbor that's been used as an open sewer since long before H.T.'s time. Under the present plan, a pipe will take treated effluent out into Massachusetts Bay, not far from the federally designated whale sanctuary. Not pleased with the plan and its potential ramifications, Cape Codders in response formed an advocacy group whose acronym is also the verb summarizing their intent: S.T.O.P. (Stop The Outfall Pipe).

A dilatory sun's rays turned the sky above and beyond the city salmon pink and pearl gray, the crepuscular sky wearing the colors of Easter morn. Below, the soft waters of the inner harbor quivered like a bowl of orange Jell-O. For no particular reason, I wandered to the stern, showing my back to the city. The 180-degree turn transported me away from late twentieth-century Boston in an instant.

The passing storm had lingered in the ship's wake, and the east was argentine. In the receding distance, island lighthouses splayed incandescence to pierce a luminous gloom, as lighthouses have throughout time. An Outward Bound crew muscled their whaleboat inward bound with straining oars, engines unchanged since antiquity, while farther astern an old catboat canted before a freshening wind, guided by the same forces of nature that propelled Ulysses, Saint Brendan, Leif Ericsson, and Christopher Columbus. Watching the ageless maritime vignette unfold in wavering light behind a transparent curtain of fog and rain, I felt for a moment like a time traveler, peering through a porthole from which history's heavy draperies had briefly parted.

We slid by Castle Island and the container docks on one side of the harbor entrance, Logan Airport on the other, the incoming big jets screeching overhead so closely I could almost reach up and touch their bellies. Only at the last possible moment before docking did any real semblance of the old city come into view, the Old North Church looking small and insignificant just beyond the downtown towers.

Rivers of ink have been expended on the popular topics of Cape Cod's explosive growth and rapid change, but far less attention has been paid to Boston's radical transformation over the years. Could that be because the city has not really changed in essence, just in its outward aspects?

Upon his arrival at Long Wharf from Provincetown in 1849, Thoreau commented that "whoever has been down to the end of Long Wharf, and walked through Quincy Market, has seen Boston . . . the more barrels, the more Boston. The museums and scientific societies and lyceums are accidental." In his view, the city existed primarily to serve one end: the propagation of commerce. In pursuit of this end, Boston has never really changed, its infinite potential for growth never altering its inherent nature. The more barrels, the more Boston. The more stories, the more square feet of office space, the more software, the more Boston. Whether 1849 or 1999, the city at heart is the same.

On the other hand, questions about Cape Cod's future are troubling in that we cannot say, "the more cottages, the more Cape Cod"; we might even say, the more cottages, the *less* Cape Cod. Unlike Boston, which has an almost limitless capacity to expand vertically, the Cape has finite limits, toward which it is approaching. How it deals with its impending limitations is unsettled, and unsettling to contemplate.

As the *Provincetown II* bumped and scraped along Commonwealth Pier, passengers jostled to be first in line at the exit ramp, some evincing the clawing, panic-stricken air of MBTA riders trapped in the rush-hour crowd when their stop arrives. Only three hours before, I myself had been concerned about timetables, but now that I was back in the city, I realized I wasn't ready to resume its pace.

In no hurry to go anywhere, then, I stayed on deck, looking ahead, looking back. In a month I'd return to the Cape to finish H.T.'s 1849 walk: I'd cover the stretch from Cahoon Hollow to Highland Light, and thoroughly explore the Provincetown dunes. In retrospect, I could see that I'd been a bit arrogant in thinking that I could duplicate Thoreau's journey in one abbreviated weekend. Not only had I overestimated my own prowess, but I'd underestimated the beach's physical demands.

In the meantime I'd be chained to my office desk, like Thoreau back home in Concord holding "a gill of Provincetown sand in my shoe," and I'd also be marking off the calendar like a kid waiting for Christmas vacation. I doubted I'd get much quality work accomplished over the next few weeks; my body would be in attendance, but my heart and mind would not—I hadn't brought them home with me. They were still somewhere out on the shores of Cape Cod, securely clamped in the jaws of a voracious beach.

Part Two

KAROL B. WYCKOFF

Uncle Tims Bridge

Columbus Day

KAROL B. WYCKOFF

Bowed Roof Cape House

7

The Cape Again

The annals of this voracious beach! Who

could write them, unless it were

a shipwrecked sailor?

CAPE COD

It was the Friday afternoon of Columbus Day weekend, raining steadily. I had had enough foresight to bring an umbrella with me to work, but then I left it behind in my haste to clear out of the office and catch the last bus making connections to the Outer Cape. My boss gave me the raised eyebrow when I wished everyone a great weekend at 4:15, but for once I was undaunted and kept moving for the door: I'd already promised to be back Monday (the holiday) to work on a big office project. Why was it that H.T. never seemed to have a problem getting away from his job at the Thoreau family pencil factory for his many jaunts?

I barely made it to South Station for the 4:30 departure after a slip-sliding sprint over Downtown Crossing's wet brick pedestrian walkway. I had to catch this bus in order to complete my walk and still make the season's penultimate Provincetown-Boston boat on Sunday. Thoreau always returned from his Cape trips by the Provincetown boat, and I was determined to stick to the tradition.

The bus was late, tied up in the early rush-hour snarl. All around horns blared, and the streets were in gridlock. The queue for the Cape snaked around the terminal and beyond the shelter of bays where buses loaded. I contemplated my recently purchased rain slicker, which had to be one of the most counterproductive pieces of clothing ever devised. It stopped well above the knee, letting my legs get a good soaking, while the hood had a ridiculous visor that came to a peak right in front of my eyes, half blinding me and conveniently funneling rain into my face and down my collar.

As we waited in line, a Munchkin-sized woman ahead, about thirty, turned around and spoke to me.

"Do you live in here?" she asked.

I pulled back my hood to expose an ear. "I beg your pardon?"

"Do you live in here?" she repeated.

I had no idea what she was talking about.

"My sister lives in here, in here Boston. I was just visitin'."

"Oh, I'm sorry," I said. "I didn't get . . . yes, I'm a Bostonian."

With no further prologue, she launched into the story of her life. It was a Cape Cod story, full of woe, naturally, but one that also testified to the indigenous moxie. She lived with elderly, infirm parents in a backwoods Mashpee cottage. Trying to better herself, aiming for a decent job off-Cape, she'd struggled for years before finally getting an associate's degree at the 4 Cs, and until recently had been driving her old AMC Pacer to a college outside Boston to audit a single course, a staggering daily odyssey. The car eventually succumbed to the grind—a broken timing belt, an oil warning light ignored, a seized engine, a car ruined, a dream deferred if not dead. She wanted to be a paralegal but was stuck inside of Mashpee with the Cape Cod blues again. "Can't go nowhere now," she said sadly, "except on the bus."

While I greatly admired her spirit I found her doleful mien depressing, and when we finally boarded I was relieved to find only single, scattered seats left. The brief random encounter ended as unceremoniously as it began: "Good-bye and good luck," I said lamely. I felt like a chump, but simply could not muster more inspirational parting words. I must work on that.

The rain let up as we headed down the Expressway, and the sky even brightened for a time. The clocks weren't scheduled to fall back for another couple of weeks, and there was enough daylight saved for me to admire autumn's influence on the deciduous forests north of piney Plymouth. The trees were generously colored, and it was a vintage foliage, I would venture, the pigments not at all delicate but deep and rich. It was as if God had commissioned an abstract expressionist to render this year's color scheme.

The day departed abruptly, as it so often does this time of year, no twilight glow softening the passage into night. Inside the bus all was quiet as we passed over the darkened Cape Cod Canal. A few people switched on overhead lights, for comfort's sake, I imagine, since they didn't have reading material. There's a unique luminescent quality to Cape Cod's peninsular atmosphere by day—the legendary "Cape Light," much admired and sought by artists—but let us put in a word also for the Cape's extraordinary darkness. The lonely cottage dweller knows it well; the driver plunges into it only two or three turns off even the most traveled roads: "Cape Nocturne," a night blacker than you imagined possible, an utter void to which the eyes never quite adjust, the world as it must have been at three o'clock the morning before Creation. A native of the city, I for one found the Cape Nocturne unnerving. "Are modern folk, perhaps, afraid of night?" Henry Beston asked. Perhaps.

The province thrust east and ahead of North America lends itself to a wide range of atmospheric shadings and colorations, including one nuance that could be a fusion of Cape Nocturne's shadow and Cape Light's clarity—call this Cape Chiaroscuro, or better yet, Cape Gothic. In between the autumnal and vernal equinoxes especially, on those sulky, silvery days when the pines are restless, the seas are troubled, and the sky holds a tacit threat, lonelier locales take on a foreboding air suggestive of scenes depicted on the covers of bodice-rippers. Not for nothing have writers ranging from Norman Mailer to Mary Higgins Clark and Marie Lee exploited desolate Cape Cod as a setting for dark tales of evil and madness.

Other media have also discovered that Cape Cod provides an ideal backdrop for the mystery thriller. Locally, there has been a successful revival of the noir-ish radio dramas of the 1930s and 1940s, with the Cape itself playing a strong supporting role. After all, what place offers better sound effects for radio—the crash of storm-churned waves, the conspiratorial whisperings of moors, the dolorous chanting and unearthly keening of foghorns in counterpoint?

Soon we were approaching Hyannis. In folds of Mid-Cape ridges, down in roadside gullies, scarlet forsythia and sumac glowed lowly in the gloaming, like banked campfires of a tribe not yet returned from the hunt. At each commuter stop we had shed passengers until by Hyannis not a suit remained. Those staying aboard or embarking at Hyannis were mostly working-class people headed for the Lower Cape; few riders appeared to be on holiday.

After we left Hyannis, the driver, a short, stout man in his thirties, bellowed out an announcement in an accent that a voice and articulation coach might term Standard Down Cape/Down East American English: "I'm gonna beeyawn vacation faw the next few weeks, so theyawl be a new drivah. Now, he won't know allya pickup stops, so make shoowah ya step out onto the road so he'll know yaw theyah."

As we headed down Cape on 6A, people got off and on the bus at obscure country crossroads or in front of cottages, never at the places listed in the P&B schedule. Past the posted Orleans stop, our Yankee Ralph Kramden pulled in at the boarded-up Dairy Queen, scene of my most excellent Labor Day greasy repast, and for a moment I thought something might be wrong with the engine. No, the driver had spotted one of his regulars waiting in the pitch dark, a young woman juggling laundry, groceries, and two toddlers. "Why're you so late?" she asked wearily as she boarded and sank into a front seat. On the outer Cape there are no chain groceries between Orleans and Provincetown, and, because of water quality issues, no laundromats at all beyond Orleans. Further, public transportation is spotty at best. To be poor and without wheels down Cape is definitely no picnic.

Taking no chances this time, I'd booked a room in advance at a Wellfleet B&B (tomorrow's walk would take me from Cahoon Hollow to Highland Light). I got off at Town Hall and headed across the street to the Lighthouse for supper. The restaurant was crowded with a predominantly male, flannel-shirted clientele. Parked along the street outside were a half-dozen pickup trucks, every single one of which had a large dog tethered in the back.

The Lighthouse was enjoying a noisy supper rush. Around one

table by street-fronting windows a bunch of young men were having a boisterous conversation, along with copious rounds of beers. Next to them a mute elderly couple huddled over Manhattans.

The other half of the small room was crowded with entire clans out for an evening or stopping by for a quick one, the scene reminiscent of rural Ireland, where pub going is a family affair. Everywhere squealing kids ran slithering under the waitresses' legs while their parents ate, drank, and gossiped. Every now and then the kids would take a break and tug at their daddies, who occasionally would pause to give pats, kisses, and quarters. The Lighthouse advertised a wide selection of beer, but almost all the adults were drinking Bud. And smoking.

As had been prearranged, I called my hostess after dining, and she was there to pick me up within five minutes. Blond-haired and in her late forties, Judy was a talker, and in moments we were chatting like old friends. By the time we had crossed over Route 6 and reached her place in the woods off Long Pond Road on the edge of National Seashore property, we were exchanging details of our lives.

Judy and her husband, Warren, were both from off-Cape. Warren had moved to this property in the 1960s to fulfill a dream of running a working farm on Cape Cod. He tried hard but gave it up when their kids (now grown and scattered) started becoming too attached to animals whose destiny was the Dartmouth slaughterhouse. Instead, husband and wife turned the place into a B&B called Winterwood Farm. Their present residence, with three guest rooms, was the farm's eighteenth-century barn, beautifully renovated.

Over a glass of wine in the cozy living room, with her ancient golden retriever slumped at my feet, Judy and I continued our conversation and were shortly joined by Warren, older than his wife by a decade. Craggy featured and rough-hewn, he had a glint of warm humor in his eyes. He'd been a Wellfleet selectman and had held other posts in town.

We talked about the Seashore and the fairly new (1990) county land use and planning agency—the Cape Cod Commission—and like many on the outer Cape with a background in real estate and development, Warren viewed both entities with a jaundiced eye. This reaction was typical of the fiercely independent people who inhabit the Cape's distant boroughs, many of whom feel hemmed in by the Seashore, which now owns much of the land, and constricted by the commission, which regulates the rest. Men of the old school, like Warren, who seal deals with a handshake over a round at the Chequessett Club, naturally chafed at what they considered to be government interference.

Thoreau wrote that government "never furthered any enterprise, but by the alacrity with which it got out of its way." I agree in certain instances—I'm no proponent of big, bureaucratic government—but I make an exception in other cases, such as protecting the Cape and its environment. There's still lots of money to be made developing what's left here, and for every honest developer there seems to come an equally sleazy one. The Cape Cod Commission is indeed an extra layer of government, but given the high stakes, it hardly imposes an onerous burden on those determined to build on the precious land remaining.

When I presented my views to Warren, he admitted that things were not always done by the book in the old days, giving me a wink and an engaging, roguish smile. Judy, who was aware that the presence of the National Seashore only helped their business, weighed in on the side of the federal government: "Let's face it, if it wasn't for the National Seashore, Ocean View Drive would look like Miami Beach." Case closed.

By this point I was not surprised when Judy and Warren expressed amazement and admiration at my efforts to recreate H.T.'s walk, and as usual when they heard a book might be involved, the stories flowed, with no prodding at all from me. I don't know that I come across as someone who would make a good listener, but when I mentioned my project people opened up without fail; native or washashore, it made no difference. I believe the fabled taciturnity of Cape Codders has gone the way of Jeremiah's Gutter, and is now just a folk memory.

Judy seemed especially concerned that I get a complete, realistic view of Wellfleet life as seen by a year-rounder, and she spoke to me as a tutor might to a willing student. A staggering number of year-rounders, she said, depended on public or private assistance to get by in winter. Among other projects, Judy coordinated an outer Cape food pantry that blanketed the region from Orleans to Provincetown, helped organize baby showers for unwed expectant mothers, and visited and took food to elderly shut-ins. One winter the economy was so bad that her group had to scrounge to buy Christmas presents for hundreds of children who otherwise would have gone without. How appropriate, I thought upon hearing this tale, that in the land which begat the Christmas Tree Shops, Santa had such industrious helpers in Wellfleet.

Judy spoke of the region's imprisoning isolation, of one elderly woman she knew who'd never been "up" Cape beyond Chatham. The woman sounded like an anachronism left behind from the old Cape Cod Henry Kittredge wrote about in the 1920s and 1930s, but there were also young people who had never been up Cape past the mall in Hyannis, Judy said, who found themselves wallowing in loneliness and depression, which even Wellfleet's frenetic summer activities couldn't help alleviate.

The Cape does seem to exert a gravitational pull on many of its residents equal to the force that causes Cape Cod's diurnal tides, except this tide flows only one way. Cape old-timers have proudly told me, "Haven't been over the bridge in twenty years." This provincial attitude is a modern phenomenon; in clipper ship days Cape Cod mariners were familiar figures in the world's seaports.

A reluctance to venture off-Cape is not limited to old salts or the poor, either. When I worked in Hyannis, I was the envy of my co-workers because I went to Boston every Friday for a weekend job. "So what in the world's stopping you from getting off-Cape once in a while?" I'd ask my colleagues, unencumbered college grads fairly new to the area. You'd think coming here they'd crossed the Rubicon instead of the Cape Cod Canal.

After talking to my hosts some more, I went to my room in the former hay loft, which was decorated with pictures of livestock from Warren's brief tenure as a gentleman farmer. The pictures reminded me that old Newcomb, Thoreau's Wellfleet Oysterman, kept a cow for milking and that his house was nearby. As H.T. tried to sleep that October night in 1849 at Newcomb's, he could not distinguish between the sound of the ocean and that of the wind; tonight, listening at an open window, neither could I.

I crawled into bed. Moments later a light pattering noise began up on the roof, shortly increasing in intensity. The sounds of sea, breeze, and now rain mingled to become one ambient voice, softly hushing *sssbhh,* and I was dead to the world in a minute.

When I awoke, it was still raining. For Thoreau's breakfast the Wellfleet Oysterman had dished out "eels, buttermilk cake, cold bread, green beans, doughnuts, and tea." Judy served me fruit salad, muffins made with freshly picked native cranberries, and coffee. Where were my eels? I asked Judy as I told her what

Thoreau had been served. Laughing, she explained that if a B&B serves what are considered "full" or hot breakfasts, it passes into a whole new regulatory domain. Such service requires a victualer's license, assures unannounced visits from health inspectors, and puts the enterprise in a different tax bracket. "Not worth the hassle," she said. "But then again, you poor guy, you've got such a long way to walk . . . no cooked eels, but I could whip you up some bacon and eggs."

"Oh, no," I said, holding up a hand. "Don't break any laws on my account."

While Judy busied herself making another batch of cranberry muffins for her weekend guests, I waited for the rain to let up with a second cup and a newspaper. The morning *Cape Cod Times* was still in the mailbox at the end of the road, so I scanned the previous day's edition instead. In a vacation mode, I didn't care much one way or the other.

A front-page story about two men believed missing off Provincetown piqued my interest. Brave Provincetown men still do battle with the sea and sometimes lose, but this particular story was hardly the stuff of heroic epic—these two fellows seemed to have vanished somewhere between MacMillan Wharf and the breakwater a few hundred yards away, not exactly the Bermuda Triangle. From all indications, they had had an accident taking a small outboard to an abandoned trawler, where one of them was living as a squatter.

A reporter had unearthed an array of minutiae concerning the men's backgrounds, all of which the *Times* saw fit to print, so that the account of their disappearance read like an exchange of gossip over a backyard fence. Employed as both fishermen and carpenters (that's the Cape Cod way), the missing pair were, according to the paper, notorious figures along the waterfront, who even before the apparent accident had been men overboard, floundering in seas of trouble, caught up in tempests of their own making. The paper duly reported rumors of their involvement in a brawl aboard another fishing boat, that their drifting skiff contained "a half-filled bottle of rum" and that one man was HIV-positive.

Despite evidence pointing to a capsizing under the influence, the men's reputations were such that there were still doubts. One line in the paper read: "It seemed conceivable to some that [the missing] left town on a binge." I put the paper down, thinking that while the men's whereabouts might be a mystery, their lives were no longer same—the indiscretions of those two sorry souls were now public record, and whether they were ultimately lost or found, their ignominious story would live on forever in the morgue of the *Cape Cod Times*.

The rain stopped. I paid for my "entertainment" and said goodbye to my most hospitable hostess, promising to return sometime. I moseyed down the farm's long dirt driveway, a rutted path with a history: it was a segment of the Old King's Highway, one of those remaining bits and pieces of the old road that still can be found on the outer Cape past Orleans. At Long Pond Road I turned right face to the beach and walked past the few private homes adjacent to federal property. The overcast sky was brightening, and the wet road was a silvery ribbon winding through oak and pine woods. On the forest floor brilliantly bronzed ferns, looking like breastplates of ancient warriors, flashed sharply through the dim arboreal light.

Cahoon Hollow is multileveled. From atop Ocean View Drive you look down on the Beachcomber Club, which in turn sits on the edge of a bluff seventy feet above the beach. The Beachcomber was boarded up for the season, but I lingered by its deserted back deck for a few moments, taking in an incomparable view of the Great Beach and the sweep of ocean beyond.

Before the Cape Cod Canal opened in 1914, before the inception of modern navigational equipment, this treacherous coast was the world's most shipwreck-prone, claiming literally thousands of vessels, thousands of lives. "Think of the amount of suffering a single strand has witnessed!" H.T. morbidly marveled. Leaning against a weathered wall of this old Life Saving Station, now a seasonal ginmill, watching big green waves roll like lengths of pipe across sandy shallows onto the voracious beach, I thought of last night's conversation with Judy and the news in the morning paper. The Cape, I reflected, can still be a treacherous place for those attempting to maneuver through the shifting bars and hidden shoals of modern life. Here you can put all America behind you, but not its distresses; the global village cannot be locked and gated.

The slice of Cape life Judy had presented me the previous evening was not unknown to me, though I appreciated her personal perspective. As a journalist I'd witnessed firsthand that the tenor of late twentieth-century life on the Cape, no less than anywhere else, has become increasingly dysfunctional. Here as elsewhere society has gone adrift, the once-strong anchor chains of family, community, and church no longer able to hold against a rising storm of societal dislocation. On the Cape alcoholism is pandemic. Poverty remains mean, persistent. Social services are a growth industry.

Crime is also a mounting concern. In H.T.'s day the circuit court would come to Barnstable County and find nothing to do because "there was not a single criminal to try, and the jail was shut up." Now the three district courts (one added recently to meet demand) are among the busiest in the Commonwealth, and the county jail has been an overcrowded tinderbox for years. Trouble in Paradise? Yes indeed, though many who should know better are often in denial. The Boston media, for instance, usually greet stories about crime on the Cape, including the geographically indiscriminate explosion of domestic violence, with incredulity.

Those who do acknowledge problems generally believe that the Cape's modern woes have swept in with the waves of "washashores." There is certainly some basis for this speculation; for all those who move or retire to Cape Cod with their lives and finances in order, there are others who come in flight, seeking to escape bad situations elsewhere, unhappy adults perhaps spurred by childhood memories of the Cape as a place of joyful sanctuary. Believing they can check their troubles at the Bourne or the Sagamore, desperate dreamers—battered single mothers, laid-off construction workers, detox alumni—are unprepared for some harsh realities: the cost of living is steep (contrary to popular belief, even off-season rents are high), and decent jobs are few and far between. And although the isolation beckons invitingly to those who have lost their compass and hope to rediscover it in solitude, it can be like a mooncusser's lantern, eventually luring the susceptible into dangerous channels. With little in the way of diversion, how easy it becomes to fall into old destructive habits.

But the Cape's contemporary social ills are not all imported; there is homegrown product as well. Read a police blotter today and it does not take long to locate proud surnames borne by the First Comers, names known to Thoreau and listed in *Cape Cod*. I don't know that the nature of the Cape Cod boy has changed all that much since 1849, when the courts and jails went wanting for business; rather, young men aren't abroad sowing their wild oats in Halifax or San Francisco or Shanghai anymore—they're home from the sea, for good, and as young men are apt to do, they often find trouble.

The sun came out, quickly dispatching the clouds and warming the air enough to let me hike in shirtsleeves. September and October can be glorious months on Cape Cod, just rewards for those who stick it out here year round—clement days, cool blanket nights, the bounty of surf and turf at peak plump, amenities that would make even a southern Californian green with envy. The big engine that's the Atlantic, slow to warm up in spring, is slow to cool down in fall, dictating the most delightful autumns, an encouraging precedent for someone who recently observed his fortieth birthday. On that upbeat note, I headed down the foot-worn path from the Beachcomber to the beach. There would be no suffering on this strand today—like nudity, vehicles, kite-flying in nesting season, and metal detectors, it was not permitted.

KAROL B. WYCKOFF

Ballston Beach, Truro

8

Peculiar and Superior

We might have made more of the Bay side,

but we were inclined to open our eyes widest

at the Atlantic. We did not care to see those

features of the Cape in which it is inferior or

merely equal to the mainland, but only those

in which it is peculiar or superior.

CAPE COD

The day had turned out so crystalline that the very molecules of air seemed to effervesce, and I felt as if I were suspended in a Nebuchadnezzar of the world's finest Champagne, and then floating through it, for the rain had packed down the sand and walking was almost effortless. It dawned on me that I now knew exactly what I'd be doing Columbus Day weekends for the rest of my life.

Between Cahoon and Newcomb hollows, the beach showed me a different look than stretches farther south. The most noticeable change was the distance between the shoreline and the bank's foot, which was much narrower. Having never hiked here before, I wasn't sure if this was caused by higher-than-average seasonal or monthly tides, or if it was the normal configuration.

I hadn't covered more than a hundred yards when just ahead a wave spilled to within ten feet of the bank. A thrill of alarm shot through me, and my heart began pounding. In *Cape Cod*, H.T. tells of three boys caught at a crumbling bank edge and buried alive in just such a surge. Fortunately for me, the sea quickly retreated, granting me the pathway. This was my only close call all day, which was surprising because the distance between water and bank was such that I often walked in the cliff's shadow. On this narrow strand where the bend in the bared arm becomes quite pronounced and the bank juts out almost to water's edge like the prow on an Admiral Dewey dreadnought, the vista of beach ahead was often less than a hundred yards.

The texture of the sea cliff past Cahoon Hollow was also some-what changed from that to the south; the slope was less vegetated and much smoother, having the raked and rolled look of a base-ball infield between innings. In brilliant sunshine the cliff was lion-colored. The gulls were out in force, acting dopey as ever, many of them perched on the wall face, pointing every which way but out to sea. Their big white and black bodies listed crazily toward the beach, and it looked as if they might tumble over and roll down at any time. I had to chuckle at how silly they looked and yet I admired their excellent balance and grip; a human standing at that sharp angle would have to perform a glissade or a stutter-step just to stay upright, but the gulls remained rock still.

Higher on the bank were a number of shelflike outcroppings (on a few of which gulls had arranged themselves like knick-knacks), as well as a ridge of horizontal grooves layered and flaking like a napoleon pastry. As usual the bank's summit, as seen from the beach, appeared flat as a table, and again the cliff's coloring and formation made me think of the American West.

The bright, crisp day was heavily scented with brine, which quickly led my mind out of the desert. Waves tattooed the beach lustily, dissolving into fizzy spume that went *pop pop pop* like spring buds opening, releasing more of the ocean's perfume. Well in front of me plumped-up waves shellacked the shoreline with big brushing motions, applying a glossy strip of sea lacquer to the sand that dulled and dried almost before the waters started to recede. No matter, the surf would lay down another coat, and another, endlessly.

Strolling along, I stumbled upon the oddest little structure, a makeshift hut set back near the bank, and I stopped to investigate. The walls of the "hut" (more like a lean-to) had been formed by driving driftwood into the sand; the roof consisted of two or three boards weighted down by flotsam and jetsam. The interior was a rough and rustic approximation of the typical Cape cottage living room or den, with old netting on the walls, colored glass and seashells set on rude shelves, and a lobster pot serving as a table—the kind of decorations you can buy new at the Christmas Tree Shop or pick up second-hand on the beach. Although it resembled something children would construct in the backyard and looked like it would not last through the first big autumn northeaster, the hut had obviously not been built in a day, or for just a day.

Like many Cape homes it came with a name: "Fort Boat du Monde" was spelled out on a handwritten sign. I puzzled over who might have built the hut, and for what purposes. Adding to my bafflement was the hut's tiny size, six feet by eight feet at the most, an extremely modest layout given the broad stretch of empty beach. It seemed too small to be a party place, and I doubted that it belonged to surf fishermen, who like to move around (and would never advertise a good spot so blatantly). The hut's occupants had left not a single clue as to their identity, with the possible exception of a bumper sticker plastered on one rough wall: "Free Leonard Peltier—Support Native Rights."

There was an offshore breeze, and into its teeth Neptune's wild stallions charged again. Today, with the sun out and at the optimum angle, the horses' manes were, in H.T.'s words, "rainbow-tinted." The spray's prismatic markings were incredibly vivid, and when the wind-driven plumes at last settled in the trough back of the incoming, I was almost taken aback to see they left no iridescent stain on the ocean surface. For one magical moment Mother Nature's sleight of light had fooled me into forgetting that the rainbow tints were not substantive, but evanescent.

Between Newcomb Hollow and Ballston Beach there's a break in the Great Wall of Cape Cod at Brush Hollow, or Brush Valley. As the cliff descended, remnants of a former settlement were exposed, old pipes mostly, jutting out from the bank top. I guessed that these belonged to homes lost, moved, or condemned long ago. In some places flattened snow fences were unfurled down the bank, and though it would have taken some doing, I could have used one like a ship's ladder and climbed right off the beach.

In the middle of the break, well back of the high-water mark, sat a large boulder, an unusual sight on this mostly rock-free coast. Greenish gray, sharp-edged, and jagged, the boulder looked like something quarried from the great granite deposits of Cape Ann, and I thought it must be a glacial erratic. But when I touched it I found it wasn't a "real" rock at all; it was a huge, hard glob of clay. As I would discover, this was a prelude of things to come.

Ballston Beach, Truro. Running westerly toward the bay is the narrow corridor of the Pamet River Valley, the river's headwaters just a stone's throw from the Atlantic's foamy clutches. In just the past few years there have been an extraordinary number of killer storms generally seen but once in a generation, furious monsters hurling great slabs of iron-colored ocean against the flimsy defenses of the narrow sand barrier separating ocean and river. In at least one instance Ballston suffered a dreaded "blowout"; this is the term used when the barrier is breached by ocean, which is analogous to an army's penetration of the enemy's rear area. But at Ballston the center has regrouped and held, denying the ocean its long-anticipated linkup with the Pamet, an occurrence that would make Truro and Provincetown island towns because the river flows into the bay. Today the barrier beach was wide and stable; the snow fences protecting the blowout area seemed almost superfluous.

H.T. took time out to explore the Pamet River Valley, one of the more interesting features of the Lower Cape. I had wandered about the area at some length on assignment years back, when the valley was the focus of a minor but telling clash between conflicting views of Cape Cod's future. The dispute pitted a septuagenarian doctor—tall, silver-maned, aristocratic, the former chief of medicine at a major Boston hospital now retired to the Truro woods—against a younger man, a feisty fellow with a long Cape pedigree, proprietor of the last working farm on the outer Cape.

The doctor, who was chair of the Conservation Committee, had proposed that the Pamet River and its environs be designated a special protected zone, to preserve its relatively pristine, undeveloped watershed. The farmer protested. A tributary of the Pamet, little more than a trickle from a river little more than a brook, crossed his land, and he feared that the Pamet's protected status would extend to his farm and perhaps restrict its uses.

One day the farmer and I stood overlooking his land from an

adjacent grassy hill, one of Cape Cod's highest points. In the valley below, cattle grazed in a deep green pasture. It could have been Vermont, except that Cape Cod Bay's gentle waves lapped along the field's western perimeter, like cows at a salt lick. The Pamet's "tributary" ran through it, and the farmer confessed that his utmost concern was that a river protection zone would encumber his ability to develop his prime parcel: he also owned the promontory from which we looked down upon the last bit of acreage in this part of the world dedicated to husbandry.

The farmer had a dilemma common among old Cape families. "I got kids, and they want to stay on the Cape," he had said, going on to tell me that the nonpareil piece of real estate on which we stood was his ace in the hole—if it became necessary, he would sell off the high ground to the highest bidder so that his children could buy houses in the hollows of Truro. Directly behind us on even loftier heights, a handful of homes had already gone up, elaborately constructed displays of wealth and ego often left empty except during August. I understood the farmer's patriarchal impulses perfectly, but I hoped he could somehow manage it so that this virgin meadow, alpine-like under a warm summer sun, would never feel the heavy tread of the Caterpillar or the bite of the Bobcat.

Ballston Beach held the usual coterie of surfcasters, sunbathers, and hundred-yard strollers, all taking advantage of the fine weather. For the fishermen, it was a dogfish day afternoon—no stripers, no blues, just sand sharks, sand sharks, sand sharks. The gratitude of all New England awaits the individual who comes up with a palatable recipe for that ubiquitous pest, *Squalus acantius*.

Taking a break, I sat down in the sand to eat an apple Judy had packed for me. An elderly couple, dressed for winter, approached and asked if I could identify the breed of ducks floating about two hundred yards offshore. "Here, you'll want to use these," the woman said, handing me a pair of binoculars.

It pleased me to think that I looked like someone who might know ducks. In fact, since my last trip I'd been devouring any material on nature I could get my hands on, books about birds, trees, the sea, whatever. I'd decided that if we're to coexist peacefully with nature, it might be nice to know our neighbors' names. Like a child, I'd become totally absorbed by a burgeoning curiosity, apt to interrupt walks with my dog or luncheon strolls through the Boston Common to look and point: "What's that?"

The biggest thrill was discovering the names and nature of common, familiar objects, such as "mermaids' purses," those little black rectangular items with the two hooked appendages fore and aft seen everywhere on the beach, which have always reminded me of an emperor's sedan chair. I'd been picking them up and studying them since I was a kid, never realizing they were the egg cases of skates.

I took the glasses and peered seaward in an attempt to attach a name to the raft of ducks. Before I could, I caught a glimpse of a large flight of birds way out to sea (was that the preferred migratory route?). Then, in the blink of an eye, they were gone. I kept searching and searching but never found them again. You can never fully grasp the huge scope of the ocean until you try to locate something upon its vastness, as any Coast Guard rescue pilot would be the first to acknowledge.

I lowered the binoculars. It was difficult to focus on the bobbing fowl, but I stayed with them and got a fix at last. "Red-breasted mergansers," I told the bird-watching couple authoritatively.

"Are you positive?" the fellow asked me.

Yes, I was. I'd done my homework, complete with my own system of mnemonics. The birds had the appropriately colored plumage, but the clincher was that wild Don King hairstyle, which will give mergansers away every time.

The bank goes back into a steep climb immediately at Ballston's edge, the heights commanded by two large gray-shingled oceanfront homes, rarer than big rocks along the National Seashore coast. If film moguls ever decide to remake *Mr. Hobbs Takes a Vacation* and shoot it here, these two homes would make prime settings, for they conjure up what I imagine must be the idealized, Hollywood image of Old Cape Cod and its soft summer dreams, a fantasy scenario in which every home has a view of the sea and the front yard is the beach.

A few paces and solitude was ushered in again. There was another beach hut, this one with a snow fence for a roof. Like the other it was neat as a pin, as if the owner had been expecting company, but there was no company (unless you count me) and no greeting host at the door, just emptiness.

Empty as well was the broad blue ocean—not a vessel to be seen, not a single dragger or lobster boat in sight. An empty beach is a wondrous thing, I think, but a desolate sea seems sad somehow. In H.T.'s day it would have been unusual to see the sea empty: "There were frequently a hundred sail in sight at once on the Atlantic." Back then, the billowing sails of the fishing fleet might have been said to float over the sea's surface like clouds, but present circumstances demanded a transposition of the simile: today, puffy clouds floated over the sea like white-plumed schooners of yore. And they sailed alone. The absence of trawlers and draggers was disturbing; the once-rich fishery off these shores has been mismanaged, by all hands, to an extent that borders on the criminal.

If the ocean had few distractions to offer, the Great Beach had not failed me yet, especially when ennui threatened to set in. The offbeat delights of these "Wonder Strands" (as H.T. believed the Vikings called Cape Cod) tend to sneak up on you, then smack you in the face. That's what happened next, as I hooked around the bank's edge at an especially narrow stretch of the littoral zone. The beach suddenly widened. At the vista's limit, about a quarter of a mile ahead, the seaward-slanting bank was a perfectly etched line against the sky, mathematically precise, as even as the hypotenuse of a right triangle drawn with a ruler, the burnished slope unmarred by brush or grass below its apex. It was as if the sea and wind had undertaken archaeologists' work to unearth half a great pyramid buried at ocean's edge. I stood staring, stunned, for some moments — the visual impact was monumental.

Passing the pyramid, I went from Egypt to Babylon, encountering a stretch of nude beach. Funny, I don't run into a soul all day, and then when I do, everyone's naked. A jovial coed crowd of about a dozen people was partying behind a windbreak, lengths of colorful cloth attached to wooden poles driven in the sand. I'd spotted a ranger nearby only recently; evidently, the National Seashore's ban against nude sunbathing is selectively policed.

Farther on, a fiftyish couple were camped out by themselves. He was stretched out in his altogether on a blanket; the woman was fully clothed in elegant attire — silk scarf, Irish knit sweater, white slacks, even sandals — and seated, reading, in a chaise lounge. I walked closer to the surf out of respect for the sunbather's privacy, but even so he placed what appeared to be a handkerchief over his midsection as I passed by, which annoyed me — as if I'd hiked all the way out here to take a gander at him.

Ahead a large black dog materialized out of a small hollow and went bounding for the surf. H.T. had laughed at the dogs he encountered on the beach, commenting that "they looked out of place here, naked and as if shuddering at the vastness." Yes, dogs are insignificant looking creatures poised on the ocean's margin, but then again so am I. As the cur loped toward me it was I who shuddered, echoing Stephen Dedalus's anxious thought in *Ulysses* when he is confronted by a similar situation on Sandymount strand: "Lord, is it going to attack me?" But no, she was a friendly Lab, sniffing about me in all the usual places.

At last a ship graced the ocean roadway, a large freighter that had just passed off the tip of the Cape heading southeast, perhaps to the Mediterranean and points beyond. Even this rusty old tub cut a romantic, dashing figure, and as with all the ships at sea it was impossible not to gaze upon it and wonder: "Where did it come from? What 'half-fabulous' ports does it seek? What treasures are stashed in its hold?"

The freighter may not have been a vessel of intrigue (although I preferred to fantasize that it was a phantom freighter of dubious registry), but it was now doing an intriguing thing: it seemed to be growing larger as it drew away from the land. At the point where it should have been the size of a toy boat in the distance, it loomed as large as if it were anchored a mile offshore. The ship never did become significantly smaller; it just sort of dematerialized when it reached the horizon.

I quickly realized that I had just seen a vivid example, and the first I can ever recall experiencing, of the seaside phenomenon called "looming," wherein objects on the water grow larger, become magnified, even as they recede from the viewer's perspective. What I had witnessed was the optical illusion known as simple looming; there are other, more complex visual "tricks" associated with sandy and watery domains, all amply described in *Alongshore*, an excellent book by John Stilgoe.

Since humans began recording observations and history, writers have made note of visual peculiarities endemic to such regions as deserts, great plains, the seashore, and the broad ocean itself. In the beach realm, much has been made of what is essentially human looming, where the viewer may perceive average-sized people to be of gargantuan proportions.

H.T. had experienced this phenomenon, noting that "objects on the beach, whether men or inanimate things, look not only exceedingly grotesque, but much larger and more wonderful than they actually are." Although I had not noticed it earlier, possibly because I saw so few people, I was now on heightened alert and soon was able to confirm at least some parts of H.T.'s statement. Dead ahead was an object that at first I took for an egregious pile of trash, then the carcass of a pilot whale, then something smaller—a dead shark perhaps? It turned out to be a chunk of rock, a true glacial erratic, neither grotesque nor wonderful at close range, though unusual enough.

I had one more mile to go until Highland Light, at which point I would have covered the beach portion of Thoreau's 1849 walk. I was more or less on automatic pilot as I neared the end of the road, believing that the true Atlantic City had revealed all its best cards by now, its most peculiar and superior aspects. Then I reached the Clay Pounds, and discovered there was one more ace in the deck—the beach was about to trump itself. Although I had read about these clay deposits, the printed word had not come close to doing them justice.

This most distinctive physical aspect of the outer beach is huge and real, not an optical illusion or a figment of the imagination.

Beginning just south of Highland Light, the sea scarp is made up predominantly of heavy clay, which, after the overnight rain, was wet and pliable enough so that a potter could have made use of it immediately. Because clay is more cohesive than other soils composing the scarp, the wall here is often the steepest along the entire coast. But every now and then even cohesive clay gives way and "slumps" over, oozing down to the beach like molten lava, then spreading out.

During or after a rain may be the best time to visit the Clay Pounds. Rainwater seeps through porous soil above the bank, flowing downward to sculpt the malleable clay facing, which at this moment was deeply scored by dozens of rivulets. After exploring close up, I stepped back to the surf's edge to get the big picture.

One large stream had divided a heap of clay at the scarp's bottom into two huge paws in the *couchant* position, with smaller streams carving out toes. Above, the "unslumped" clay bank remained nearly vertical. The resulting effect was nothing less than fabulous — I was looking at the figure of a broad-breasted sphinx, minus the head.

First a pyramid, then the sphinx — where was I? Which sea was this that washed over and soaked my sneakers? H.T.'s imaginative eye looked over the ocean from this beach and envisioned the coast of Spain, "and farther yet the pillars which Hercules set up." I was almost ready to believe that Hercules' pillars lay just beyond the horizon, and if the proper atmospheric conditions for an "extraordinary" looming developed, I might yet look upon them.

I must confess that following the Labor Day hike, when it seemed as if I would never get out of the office again, I had thought briefly about skipping this eight-mile section, wrongly assuming, to paraphrase both Spiro Agnew and Ronald Reagan, that if you've seen one beach you've seen them all. I had dismissed that idea almost as quickly as it occurred to me, and now I was thankful that I had. The length of beach from Cahoon Hollow to Highland Light is indeed a superior place. I've not traveled all that extensively but I have been to Big Sur and the west coast of Ireland, and I have no qualms at all about installing Cape Cod Beach among that vaunted company.

There are natural wonders of the world here, and marvelous and strange things can come upon you like bolts out of the blue. It's all there for those who, in Beston's words, "use their eyes." A sense of whimsy is optional but highly recommended. Like humanity's finest works of art, the unfolding vistas of sea and cliff and sky are rife with allusion, and though these places need not be defined solely by our terms, it was only natural for the observer to seek out descriptive metaphors as grandiose as the visions he had beheld.

Unnoticed by me, the day had dimmed as I scouted out the Clay Pounds, and suddenly a low cloud, dark and heavy, came from the direction of the bay and surged over the top of the bank like a rogue wave. The cloud let out a few droplets of rain, and then it began to pour. It was a good thing the rain cloud grabbed my attention, for in looking up I caught a glimpse of Highland Light, or more precisely, the windowed top of the tower, just yards ahead of and above me. I'd almost missed seeing a structure sixty-six feet tall situated near the edge of a bluff 120 feet high! How could this be? Was my mind still in ancient Egypt?

I retraced my recent steps to do a check on my eyesight and attentiveness. H.T. had spotted the lighthouse from the distance of a "mile or two," but today I saw that I could be forgiven, for this circumstance had definitely changed. At no point south of the lighthouse did more than its upper extremity show, and when I retreated even farther, it disappeared altogether. Although this all seems counterintuitive, I'm sure there's an explanation. The bank at Highland Light is steep, the beach vantage point narrow, and erosion has taken about 215 feet out of the cliff since 1849. In addition, the absence of any lighthouse sighting from more than a few hundred yards back gave further testimony to the Cape's curvature, and confirmed its keeper's complaint to H.T. "that the lighthouse should have been built half a mile farther south, where the coast begins to bend, and where the light could be seen at the same time with the Nauset lights, and distinguished from them." The campaign to save the lighthouse was based on its cultural and historical value, not its utility; in any case, it was not designed to be a beachcomber's beacon.

Highland Light now behind me, I reached Coast Guard Beach, Truro. It was still raining. I emerged from the beach into the parking lot, where two gentlemen, an older fellow and a young surfcaster, both offered me rides. I declined with thanks because I still wanted to walk and explore. H.T. said of Cape Codders, "we like their manners, what little we saw of them," and I concur.

Back of the beach there commenced a rolling moor, now mystical in the light rain, its shrubbery glowing bright red and green, the colors of ships' running lights. The huckleberry plants were particularly attractive, leaves shiny red as blood and set in starburst patterns, like Fourth of July fireworks.

The bushes were all fat with fruit—huckleberry, blueberry, beach plum, bayberry. The only pickers of this rich harvest were birds and small animals, however, for those who toil in the Cape Cod cottage industries churning out beach plum jelly, homemade pies, and scented candles must seek their raw materials elsewhere—the government discourages anyone from taking commercial advantage of this public land. The general rule is that individuals may pick only as much fruit as needed for personal use. (That goes for driftwood as well.)

The path from the beach had taken me in a hook around Highland Light, and now from the "interior," at the top of Coast Guard Beach Road, it could be seen in full stature. Walking down South Hollow Road to the highway, I began to feel weary, and the sound of cars on Route 6 for once was music to my ears.

H.T. traversed the outer beach and its environs at the pace of eight to ten miles a day. I made identical progress, not so much because I intended it as because that's the way it worked out. After covering that distance over the Great Beach, you seem to reach the limit of human endurance. Modern walkers, even those in tip-top condition, should find this daily pace to be just right, for slogging ahead much farther is almost certain to bring on extreme fatigue, not to mention sensory overload.

If accommodations are in order, then, one can easily stick to H.T.'s 1849 itinerary: Day One, Orleans to Wellfleet; Day Two, Wellfleet to Highland Light; Day Three, Highland Light to Provincetown; and Day Four, Provincetown. A tour of the Provincelands can be fit into either Day Three or Four. (Thoreau spent a fifth day in Provincetown, but it was uneventful.) Because of my Labor Day lodging debacle I had to do parts of the walk out of sequence, but I maintained the spirit of the 1849 excursion, and now I had only to tramp the dunes tomorrow and this journey would be completed.

I was heading for the motel where I had stayed over Labor Day; continental breakfast or not, it was nearby and close to the only restaurant within walking distance. But there was a motel right as I emerged onto Route 6, at the junction of 6A, and wanting to get out of wet clothes quickly I decided to check it out. It was called Neptune's Hideaway. With free HBO and no telephones, it seemed perfect.

The woman in the office told me there were plenty of vacancies. The first room she showed me was just fine, but she was determined that I see a couple more. The second room was an exact replica of the first, except that the double bed was facing the other way. It really didn't matter to me whether my aching feet pointed north or south, but the woman was so earnest that I said, "No, much better, I'll take this one."

Later I went to retrieve my credit card at the motel office, and the helpful proprietor snared me for a talk. For some reason I pegged her—a fiftyish, blonde-haired woman who spoke in a slow monotone—as a burnt-out year-rounder. I was correct, but I also learned that she was well educated, and that she was from a prominent upstate New York family. She certainly was jaded about the Cape: name almost any group—her fellow washashores, the Provincetown Portuguese, gays, cops, art gallery owners—and she had a barbed comment to make.

According to her, civilization as we know it ends in South Wellfleet, and the outer Cape is as lawless as the Old West. The place was awash in drugs and booze, she said, and it might well be the spousal and child abuse capital of the United States. Most of the local law enforcement officials were utterly incompetent. I was amused (and bemused) by her solution: "Send the U.S. attorney, the U.S. marshals, and the F.B.I. down here." Boston was too far away to dispense justice, in her opinion, so the feds would have to occupy Wellfleet, Truro, and Provincetown. I take it her idea was not driven by hopes of filling up Neptune's Hideaway with government officials on expense accounts, since she didn't own the place, just ran it for a friend.

Her views were extreme to be sure, but the interesting mono-

logue snapped me out of a late-afternoon, low-blood-sugar leth-
argy, and I set off up the road for Goody Hallett's refreshed and
with an outrageous appetite. At Goody's I sat at the bar, as is my
habit. There was a college football game from the West Coast on
the tube, and I asked my neighbors, "How'd B.C. do today?" No
one, including the bartender, knew, or cared. My innkeeper had
nailed one fact dead: Boston *is* a long way from here!

As on Labor Day weekend, I was struck both by the size of
the place and by how its dimensions easily dwarfed the thin
crowd. There are more than a few restaurants like Goody Hallet's
on Route 6, but many of them seem to be chronically empty.
Goody's had the only year-round liquor license in Truro, which
helped it survive, but you could probably fit most of the local
drinkers in there and still have plenty of room to spare.

For dinner I ordered eggplant parmigiana, spaghetti, garlic
bread, salad, and wine—certainly not the traditional Cape Cod
fisherman's dinner (more like a Neapolitan fisherman's), and certainly not what H.T. would have eaten—but just the fodder to
quiet my body's clamoring for carbohydrates. Meanwhile, I
looked around and eavesdropped. The easy camaraderie among
the dozen or so customers indicated that they were regulars; I
was the only outsider present. The hot topic was what had tran-
spired at a party held recently after the big outer Cape volunteer
firemen's muster, a high point on the local social calendar. It
seems some guy had punched out his dog, after which incensed
party goers punched out the malefactor. Bar patrons who had
missed the brouhaha nodded in righteous satisfaction at the punishment meted out.

Goody Hallet's was named after a woman who, according to
Cape legend, was the lover of the pirate Sam Bellamy. Bellamy's
ship sank off Wellfleet in 1717 (and was found by treasure hunter

Barry Clifford in the 1980s, to much fanfare). Bellamy drowned, and the pirates who made it to shore were seized, taken to Boston, and hanged. Rumors have always persisted, though, that a handful of them eluded capture. The man sitting next to me tonight could have been a direct descendant of one of those lucky escapees, with his bandanna, dark straggly beard, and single big hoop earring.

The "pirate" informed me he put down tile during the day and was in a band at night, making it clear that the nocturnal pursuit was his true vocation. He was also, he said, two semesters shy of a college degree. He was a geology major, and he told me that he found the Cape a less interesting study than other parts of the country. "It's just glacial garbage," he said, with a wave of dismissal. Glacial garbage? I'd just seen the Clay Pounds, and I was highly offended.

The bartender, who was also the owner, presented my bill. With her cowboy-cut jeans, worn face, and distinctly off-Cape twang, she would not have been out of place in a sagebrush saloon, slinging Rocky Mountain oysters instead of the Wellfleet variety. Responding to my question, she said she had moved to the Cape eighteen years before from parts west.

"I thought so," I said, "it's your accent. Where out west?"

"As far as you can go west," she replied. "The Berkshires."

Back at the motel, grateful feet facing "up" Cape, I fell to sleep easily and gratefully. Around midnight, slamming car doors outside my open window and loud voices full of alcohol roused me slightly. The voices, belonging to a man and a woman, passed into a room adjoining mine, and within moments had softened into romantic coos.

I thought I was in for a long night of it, but the neighboring room went silent shortly thereafter. And there lay I ensconced in

Neptune's Hideaway, bed half empty not half filled, but no faithful Penelope held on for this Odysseus, and even my old paramours the Sirens were directing their song elsewhere these days. Just when I became concerned that thoughts of my lovelorn life would keep me awake brooding half the night, the heavens opened up again. A slight breeze stirred the curtain, and that was surely the ocean sounding in the distance. For the second straight night I was gently put under by the lullaby of my true, elemental lovers—the rain, the wind, and the fitful sea.

9

Heaven of Sand

It was as if I always met in those places

some grand, serene, immortal, infinitely

encouraging, though invisible companion,

and walked with him.

HENRY DAVID THOREAU

I was up with first light, for there was a lot to accomplish before the 3:30 P.M. boat to Boston. I slipped my room key through the office mail slot and struck out on the main road, Route 6, which would lead me directly to dune country. It was very foggy.

In no time at all I'd drawn abreast of the former East Harbor, now Pilgrim Lake. With fog concealing the high dunes on the Atlantic side of the lake, and the wind churning up a chop on the shallow lake's surface, a stranger without a map might think he had reached ocean's edge, but the Atlantic was still half a mile or so away.

I left Route 6 and moved toward the dunes by the fire gate, where tours from town enter. The path leading to the first row of dunes was brightly edged with colorful plants—purplish, flam-

boyant Joe Pye weed, stiff asters in lavender, yellow-orange but-
ter-and-eggs, and wild phlox. The phlox was a bit of a surprise,
for according to my field guide, it blossoms from April to June.
Yet there they were, no doubt about those rich delft petals,
spring's flowers granted one final stay of execution through the
beneficence of the still-temperate Atlantic.

The first large dune I encountered took the shape of an amphi-
theater, with three long, half-buried snow fences running perpen-
dicularly down its front as if demarcating aisles, like ushers'
ropes. The bowl was all sand from the orchestra section up, with
only the balcony top planted with ears of beach grass. Looking
over my shoulder, I saw no one in sight, so like a maestro at the
stand I bowed to the ghostly mists in attendance.

I next headed off for another tall dune near the highway, which
my map told me was called Mount Ararat. The fact that Ararat
has long been tracked and charted belies the fundamentally pro-
tean nature of the dunes. Thoreau himself had scaled it 150 years
ago; I also climbed to the top, possibly illegally, though I took
care not to trample any of the grasses. From its peak I could just
barely make out the outline of nearby Provincetown, which still
slumbered under the blanket of fog.

Finding no sign of an ark on Ararat, I descended and met up
again with the path carved out by decades of beach buggy travel.
From the heights of initial sandy ridges, the road snaked down
into a valley. Glimpsed through a slowly lifting mist, the dune
panorama was eerily beautiful, and the path seemed about to lead
to a place of enchantment, perhaps an oceanside Brigadoon.

I paused for a look before moving on. H.T. had seen the dunes
as "vast platters of pure sand," and I remember childhood views
of the dunes that approached something out of *Lawrence of Arabia;*
any moment Bedouins on coal black horses might have come

charging over the long white crests. But out of necessity, to save Provincetown from being buried alive, there have been plentiful beach grass plantings over the years, and grasses have taken hold across much of the terrain. This has led to further colonization by low shrubs and trees, and today greenery has come to dominate the landscape, reducing oceans of sand to narrow canals in some places, and in others encircling beige islets on the dune platters like sides of vegetables around a chop. In this case the oasis, such as it was, had begun to overwhelm the desert, although experts say the situation is fluid and speculate that the sands might yet regain the upper hand.

Down I went into the valley. Around a sharp S curve of the heavy sand path, a man suddenly appeared out of the fog. His pants were suspendered, and his long-sleeved undershirt had buttons at the top, in the style of a union suit. He wore a wide-brimmed leather hat, leather boots, and held in one hand an odd-looking wooden object, in the other a small sack. I believe my heart skipped a beat as the apparition approached; for a moment I thought I was about to have an audience with the ghost of Henry David Thoreau.

The specter turned out to be an amiable man named Peter, a longtime summer resident of North Truro, who had just completed his traditional Columbus Day rite of cranberry picking in the valley, the berries destined for a homemade sauce ("just boil 'em with sugar"), garnish for his Thanksgiving bird. The wooden contraption was an old-fashioned scoop used to pluck the cranberries out of a dry bog; the sack held about five pounds of fruit.

Had Peter picked more cranberries than for his own use, he would have been breaking the rules of the National Seashore. Peter hated the park rangers, whom he called "brownshirts," with a passion. His face darkened as he told me how he'd been ticketed the past summer for using a path to the beach formed after 1962, a violation of Seashore preservation rules. "They just won't listen to you," he sputtered. "The sand shifts and you tell them this *is* the old path, but they just won't listen."

The year 1962 is significant because it was the year following the Seashore legislation's passage and the first season the federal government actually became a force on Cape. When Peter said the words "nineteen sixty-two," he did so with the same tone of mixed sadness, anger, and regret that Europeans reserve for mention of 1914 and Southerners for 1865. In his view, the feds had destroyed the Cape Cod way of life. The Park Service had gone overboard in its efforts to help the piping plover, he said, and was using the plover as an excuse to harass off-road vehicle users. Plover numbers would always be small here because the Cape was the point of its northernmost migration; on the Jersey shore, Peter claimed, the bird was thriving even though ORV routes had remained open. Peter sneered at the plover's protected status: "I've been to China, and over there they serve plovers for dinner!"

The high point of Peter's harangue, however, came during a discussion of the beach grass–planting scheme. "It's illegal!" he said over and over, pointing to a large plantation in the direction of the Atlantic. In his view, the grassing of sands there was illegal because the area comprises what are considered "moving" dunes. "If they want to stop dunes moving toward Provincetown, they should stop them *there*"—he indicated dunes close by Route 6— "and not *here*"—his hand swept to sands stretching to the sea. "The grass has flattened out the Atlantic side dunes, and it's become an artificial plain instead of a rolling dune." The stretch in question was indeed as flat as a Kansas wheat field, an image reinforced by rippling blades of tall green-blonde beach grass.

As always I welcomed opinions like Peter's, but as always I took them with a grain of sea salt. The stupendous benefit of the National Seashore to Cape Cod needs no recounting here, and I thought his comments about Seashore personnel to be overly harsh and prejudiced. I've invariably found Park Service employees to be highly dedicated, responsible, and helpful public servants, generally overqualified and underpaid (if occasionally stiff-necked and defensive, as bureaucrats are wont to be). And the plover's protection is a matter of federal mandate, a strict legal directive over which Park Service officers in the field have no latitude.

After bidding Peter good-bye, I trekked down the winding road into Brigadoon, anticipating the spectacular "autumnal tints" of the dune interior over which H.T. had practically gushed: "I never saw an autumnal landscape so beautifully painted as this was. . . . [I]t was like the richest rug imaginable. . . . [T]hey were warmer colors than I had associated with the New England coast."

The foliage of the valley turned out to be a disappointment, however. Cape fall colors are usually described as "subtle," but today the dune bushes and shrubs were little more than dull, and except for a few strands of ground-hugging poison ivy, bright red and fairly crackling like live wires on the sand floor, there was not much that was rich or warm.

The lack of seasonal coloring was somewhat surprising following the brilliant trees I'd seen near the Cape Friday and the variegated Truro moors I'd witnessed just the day before. There were, however, compensating bursts of un-autumnal colors in the form of dazzling ivory white and sherbet pink salt spray roses: *Rosa rugosa,* that familiar, widespread, aggressive colonizer of Asian import introduced around Thoreau's time, a flower whose tinctures provided some welcome relief against the sallow features of the interior valley.

Although providing few Kodak moments for the human lens, the shrubberies were quite up to fulfilling more essential functions, for they were heavily fruited, and birds were breakfasting with gusto. Literally hundreds of swallows were feasting on berries. With their tiny wings but whirring blurs, their little heads leaning forward to nosh, the hovering swallows appeared to have taken a page out of the hummingbird handbook. Upon seeing me approach, one broke from his feeding, flew over, and delivered his calling card onto an open page of my notebook, a lavender-colored dropping holding dozens of tiny seeds, as in a jam. My huckleberry friend.

It may be that few hikers make their way out here, but that is not true of vehicles with four-wheel drive. Soon, I could hear the straining gears of the Provincetown Dune Tour fleet behind me. As the buggies-for-hire ponderously approached my position, I understood at once what Cynthia Huntington meant when she described the vast Provincetown Spit as "this trammeled wilderness."

I stepped out of the sand path to let one buggy pass, but instead it stopped, and two young men sitting in the back seat beckoned to me. Had I noticed all the swallows out on the dunes, they asked? If so, were they bank swallows or barn swallows?

Again, I was happy to be taken (or mistaken) for an expert, but I wasn't sure. Nevertheless, given that I had walked the beach from Eastham to Provincetown along twenty-eight miles of bank and had yet to run across a barn, I took a stab: "Bank swallows," I said. *"Riparia riparia."* Nonplused for a second by the Latin, one fellow jabbed his companion with an elbow as if a wager was at stake. "Thank you *very* much, sir," he called as they drove off, deflating me only slightly with the "sir."

The dune tours came along frequently, drivers slowing down often to let people give me a howdy: "Whatcha doin' way out here?" After a while I wondered if I was becoming a tour attraction myself.

Down the main path I came upon a strange edifice, a concrete building that looked like a garage except that its portals were too narrow for cars. Nearby rested a collapsed wooden structure, little more than a battered roof. Now it was my turn to ask questions. The next tour driver told me that this was the old Peaked Hill Life Saving Station, boat house and guards' living quarters, moved off the beach and unused for years. It was his dream, the driver added, to restore the station to the beach and bring schoolchildren on educational field trips. I think that someday Provincetown may become one big museum.

The buggy trail narrowed between moderate stands of oak and brush, a perfect place for ambuscade, the sand marked by pawprints of a large dog, not a creature I was looking forward to meeting out here. Then the path widened again, and beyond rose the last dune between me and sea, the ocean now clearly audible and making a sizzling sound, like bacon on a griddle. On top of the ridge nestled three dune shacks.

The pawprints on the path were from a golden retriever who belonged to two women and four young children on a day's outing to an oceanfront dune shack. The whole party was standing at the base of the dune, wrestling with a pump, trying to fill a plastic milk container with fresh well water. "Can you get this working for us?"

I wish they had asked me something I could wing, like bank swallows versus barn swallows, but a pump? It was an old-fashioned hand contraption, and I'd never worked one in my life; I wasn't even sure I understood the principle behind its operation. Yet women assume that all men come genetically programmed with the ability to do certain things automatically, and with panache—carve a turkey, jump a dead battery, or prime a pump, whatever that means—and so in the spirit of gender pride, I gave it a shot.

Pump pump pump, I went, *gurgleburp gurgleburp gurgleburrrp,* came the dry, mocking retort. I even tried kicking the pump shaft. Thoreau probably would have had the thing cranking in a second, producing enough water to make this desert bloom, but I never was able to get it started. I offered sheepish apologies and fervent wishes that the group not die of thirst, then continued on my way.

I climbed a path adjacent to the shack to check out a cottage beyond and take in an ocean view. Although posted against uninvited visitors, the beach house appeared deserted and I nosed around the property.

There were nineteen dwellings known collectively as the Dune Shacks still standing on the wilds of Provincetown Spit when I passed through. Earlier that day while wandering around in a barren hollow, I'd come across what might have been the smallest of these, a pile of wood no bigger than the security guard's sentry box at Oyster Harbors. The place by which I now stood was one of the more impressive shacks, based on its size (porch, half dormer, perhaps three large or four small bedrooms) and supreme vantage point, which offered peerless ocean panoramas. Regardless of its size, however, this dune cottage and all the others were not at all elaborate—they are literally shacks, built of wood and tarpaper. They lack electricity and must use propane or driftwood for fuel. To the disdain of their fellow rustics, two or three occupants recently added indoor plumbing.

You would not have to know the history of these weathered shacks to recognize that they are imbued with a certain romantic luster, that they have been home to the odd and offbeat, and that if those groaning old boards could talk, oh, the stories they could tell! But this is Cape Cod, this is Provincetown, where storytelling and mythmaking come as second nature, and the shacks make ideal subjects for embellishment.

For their admirers, each shack bears the aura and legacy of Eugene O'Neill, who wrote some plays while living isolated in the dunes; later he was followed by other literary figures, Jack Kerouac and Norman Mailer allegedly among them.[*] To hear some of the stories, one might think that contemporary American culture would hardly exist were it not for the existence of the dune shacks, to which, it's solemnly held, no one has ever come out just to goof off.

In fact, O'Neill's cottage was lost to a storm in 1932, at which time not one of the present shacks was built, and many of the shacks dating from the late 1930s were originally conceived of and developed as ordinary Cape Cod vacation rentals. To be certain, many important artists, especially painters and sculptors, have worked here, but the legendary literary connection has been somewhat exaggerated. One woman apparently used to host a kind of unbuckled literary salon at her shack, and over the years the roster of writers who dropped by for cocktails evolved into a list of authors who came out to labor over manuscripts. "It became sort of like 'Washington Slept Here,' " I was told. Famous

[*]There was also the poet Harry Kemp—who visiting Provincetown has not heard of Harry Kemp? Who knows who he was?

writers did come to visit, but it is highly doubtful that they actually produced major work while at the shacks.

Still, the literary legends surrounding the shacks probably helped save them in the late 1980s, when leases came up, elderly tenants started dying, and the federal government seemed intent on ridding the National Seashore of these manmade "blights." (Built on land that has always been public, the shacks came with no legal deeds or titles, unlike protected "improved properties" that were built on private lands absorbed by the government for Seashore use.) There was a widespread public hue and cry to save the shacks as irreplaceable national historic treasures, and the Park Service eventually backed down from the firestorm of criticism.

Subsequently, the Park Service agreed that remaining shack dwellers could reside either for life or for the term of a set lease. The government will use the shacks that revert to it for educational purposes, geared to artistic pursuits. A private nonprofit group already maintains a number of the cottages for artists and other interested parties, available for occupancy through a lottery system. Just as our grandchildren, then, will be able to walk the Great Beach pretty much as Thoreau did, so also will future artists always be able to find solitude and pursue creative endeavors in these rough Waldenesque huts overlooking sea and dune. As a Provincetown woman who spearheaded efforts to save the shacks once asked, "Who knows when the next O'Neill will come along?" In anticipation of that eventuality, the Park Service and the Peaked Hill Trust will leave a hurricane lantern burning in the window.

From the simple shack I turned my attention to the majestic sea. All was fairly placid, though waters close in were active as usual, with sandbars agitating the gentle but steady flow of breakers, and for a hundred yards offshore the surf bubbled and frothed like a giant Jacuzzi. Some larger waves were coming in double-decked, the upper wave riding the lower as surely as a surfer hangs ten on a board. Shallow bars split incoming waves down the middle, the two streams then curving around to meet up again, rising and butting headlong into each other like kid goats jousting. It was as if the Atlantic were in a playful mood today out at the Peaked Hill Bars, known as the "Graveyard of the Atlantic" in the days of sail, and from the exuberant shallows and surf came what sounded like strains of joyous laughter.

In her fine story "The Spiral," the writer Cynthia Huntington (who really did live and work in a dune shack) made note of the "peculiar unity" of the elemental forms constituting this wilderness. Sea, sky, and dune do seem at times to be mirror images, don't they? The sea and sky are almost always decked out in matching colors and fabrics—gray corduroy today, blue silk tomorrow—and sea and dune are both perpetually rising, falling, curving, curling, cresting, questing. Today the varied surfaces of this universe shared another common feature: the ocean, dunes, gray-clouded sky, empty beach, and even the sandy bars and sea bottom visible just offshore—all were uniformly *furrowed*, looking as if God had teasingly raked a hand through them all, His tousle-headed children.

I retraced my steps back toward town, stopping for a last look over Provincetown Spit from the high road, dredging through my thoughts in search of a concise phrase to help capture what I'd seen, what I'd experienced. Something grand was in order, for the dull foliage in the valley below and the "Kansas wheat field" ahead notwithstanding, this country had left a singular impression on the dune explorer.

Norman Mailer once wonderfully described the Provincetown

dunes as resembling "the hills of heaven." Remembering that phrase, I reached into my backpack for my copy of *Cape Cod*. There, in a chapter about the dune country titled "The Sea and the Desert," Thoreau quotes from an epic Viking poem, which he believed—contrary to historical evidence—was an account of a Norse journey past these very shores:

> Let us make a bird skillful to fly through the heaven of sand,
> to explore the broad tracks of ships;
> while warriors who impel to the tempest of swords,
> who praise the land, inhabit Wonder Strands, *and cook whales.*

H.T. provides an interpretation of the Icelanders' poetic metaphors: *bird* is a ship, *tempest of swords* is a battle, and—what's most interesting—*heaven of sand* is the sea, "which is arched over its sandy bottom like a heaven." I had recalled the expression from my reading but forgotten what it specifically signified. No matter, like a true beachcomber I decided to appropriate it anyway and fashion it for my own use. "Heaven of sand" fulfilled my need to come up with an evocative image for the dunes, fit the bill nicely, and, indeed, worked for the Great Beach in its entirety, yet I saw no reason not to include the Vikings' imaginative usage as well. I thereby anointed "heaven of sand" to be a one-size-fits-all metaphor, a multipurpose expression encompassing the beach, the dunes, *and* the ocean.

I turned from the heaven of sand for town, from which nowadays people head out to watch whales, not cook them. All morning the mist had been slowly dissipating, and at the highest point of the winding buggy path, Provincetown, earlier cloistered behind fog, suddenly sprang at me—clear, distinct, in almost unnaturally sharp focus, like a 35mm slide help up close to a bare light bulb. I could also see a helicopter probing along the harbor, tracing a line from Long Point to Beach Point, flying low, back and forth. This was no drill, I knew—they were looking for something.

In the distance, tall beach grass flickered in a moderate breeze, and it looked as if the dune rims were consumed by pale green fire, the mirage so convincing I thought I also saw it give off a clear smoke rising to the sky. Around me, more gorgeous blue phlox bloomed way out of season. Pilgrim Lake was whitecapped and luminous under gray clouds, as was Cape Cod Bay just yards to the west; the State Police chopper continued to thunder overhead. Then I noticed that the two towheaded children in a passing dune buggy had turned in their seats to stare back at me, fixated, wide-eyed. Imagine, all the intriguing natural wonders surrounding them, and they were most fascinated by some guy in ill-fitting shorts and ripped sneakers taking notes with a broken pencil, and scribbling madly in a notebook whose pages kept sticking together thanks to a little bird's indiscretion.

Now concerned about getting to the 3:30 ferry on time, I walked down the Snail Road to town at a most unsnail-like clip. Arriving in Provincetown, I found I had plenty of time to spare, and decided to stop by the Ship's Bell, a motel/inn straddling Commercial and Bradford, run by my old friends Bill and Nancy McNulty. Within minutes the three of us were sitting in the Ship's Bell's cozy common room, a fire roaring.

I had first met Bill and Nancy when I was a reporter on the Cape. Back then Bill had been Provincetown's town manager and Nancy had served on the School Committee. Both were natural raconteurs, and there didn't seem to be a single tidbit of town gossip they weren't aware of. But when I commented this morning on their encyclopedic command of Provincetown lore, Bill felt compelled to say, "You must always remember, we're *locals*, not *natives*, and will never be privy to all the secrets. Locals, not natives." They had lived here a mere thirty years.

The telephone rang. When Bill returned his face was grim and drawn. "They identified the body," he told Nancy. He turned to me and said, "A man we know drowned. They found him this morning."

"The State Police helicopter . . . ?"

Bill nodded. It turned out to be the second of the two missing fishermen-carpenters I'd read about in the paper the day before; the first body had been fished out of the harbor earlier. The McNultys were especially close to the story because out-of-state family members of the man just found—a Wellfleet resident— were staying at the Ship's Bell. In the short time it took me to walk from the dunes to town, police in the helicopter had spotted his body wedged in the rocks of the Provincetown breakwater, recovered it, and summoned the family to the Coast Guard station.

All over the Cape, gravestones eulogize native seafaring men lost in pursuit of their livelihoods—Thoreau read many such inscriptions—but what would be etched on the tombs of those lost at sea while being pursued by their demons? Like a haunting melody, a line from that earlier *Cape Cod Times* story came back to me: "Both men are known as heavy drinkers and drug users, according to family and friends." Change the tense, and you have their epitaph. O men who go down to the sea in skiffs.

The skiff's outboard motor had also drowned in the incident, but unlike men dead motors can have life breathed into them again. The Merc, which belonged to the Wellfleet man, was now in Bill's backyard, sitting in a fifty-five gallon barrel of salt water until a skilled mechanic could begin the recovery process. The salvage effort made sense; the outboard probably constituted a significant portion of its late owner's estate.

Soon after, I said good-bye to my friends and headed down Commercial Street, the pavement choked with pedestrians and baby carriages.

I had a tasty lunch at the Lobster Pot, an outstanding bowl of that local staple, kale soup. Afterward I crossed over to the Governor Bradford to catch the Patriots' score on TV. Eventually the bartender broke off his conversation with a patron and ambled over to pour me a draft. Next I headed for a bookstore where I found a new edition of *Cape Cod* to purchase. The agitated clerk almost bowled me over going to her register, snapped money for the purchase out of my hand, and threw the bag containing my book across the counter. If I have one gripe about Provincetown, it's that—contrary to its general *laissez les bon temps rouler* attitude—customer service can be breathtakingly rude.

A woman approached me outside the bookstore, and I recognized her from one of the dune groups. "Hello. My children insisted that we stop and talk with you," she said. "We've seen you walking so many places today we thought you might be twins, or triplets!" The polite boy and girl standing by her side were the same pair who had thought me such a riveting local point of interest a few hours earlier. She and her husband and preadolescent children (from Fairfield County, Connecticut) surrounded me outside the Crown and Anchor,* full of interest and rapt attention. I couldn't resist the urge to pontificate.

The arduous walk, I told them, was research for a book I was

*The legendary Crown and Anchor hotel/entertainment complex was virtually destroyed by fire in February 1998.

working on, and in way of explanation I pulled out the new edition of *Cape Cod* I'd just bought so that I could read Paul Theroux's introduction. "This is your book?" she asked, misunderstanding.

I had to laugh. "I wish." I explained what I was up to. The rest of the family was quickly satisfied, but the woman continued to pepper me with questions, for most of which I had no or only vague answers to give: "What's the title? When will it be finished? Will we be able to buy it in Darien? What's your name?" I *was* able to handle the last one.

As we parted after a few moments more of conversation, the woman turned and shouted back at me, "You hurry up and write that book, so we can read it!" At her words my shoulders momentarily sagged; it was not lost on me that the most difficult part of this journey still lay ahead.

At MacMillan Wharf I waited for the packet to begin taking on passengers. Behind the long breakwater the harbor where the lads were lost was soft gray and streaked, like brushed velour. Down the bay shore on Beach Point, buildings loomed "much larger and more wonderful" than they actually were, the long view over water abetting an illusion that had transformed each two-room cottage into Mar-a-Lago, each efficiency motel into The Breakers.

From MacMillan's end I let my gaze sweep the inner sleeve of the entire peninsula, Provincetown right around to Sandwich. Now there was a grand view: Cape Cod on a platter, dressed and laid out in full view. But a walk along the bay shore, I decided, where little is concealed, where the views are as open and obliging as those who live beside it are said to be, could never be as interesting as its Atlantic counterpart. Not only are the ocean side's physical attributes more peculiar, and superior, but its peculiarities and superiorities are revealed only gradually as you proceed from point to point on the arc's far edge; out there, there's no such concept as "getting ahead of the curve." Geography is destiny, and the geography of the Great Beach is destined to fill the walker with a sense of never-ending discovery and infinite possibility.

The day had remained gloomy and overcast even after the fog lifted, the big October clouds tattered and dirty as an old T-shirt. The boat was filled to just a third of capacity, and I had no difficulty getting a window table for myself to spread out books and notes. The sea was heavy enough to provoke small craft warnings, and when the skipper announced a possible sighting of a humpback whale off Wood End, only I and a couple of kids ventured out on the pitching deck to take a look.

The whale never showed, so I headed back indoors to the bar, where I noted again with dismay the close proximity of the unwell to the dispensary of cordiality—oh, why couldn't they take their suffering elsewhere? The face of one man prostrate on the bench was an agonized death mask, his complexion a study in chartreuses—green, yellow, and all the shades in between. His sourpuss partner was none too pleased with her Prince Charming just now; though she cradled his head in her lap, each time he moaned (which was about every ten seconds) she'd counter with an exaggerated roll of her eyes. The scene made me think of H.T.'s comment, "There is no telling what it may not vomit up," but of course he was referring to the sea, not the seasick.

I went on the outdoor deck and stood at the bow, alone, thinking of the refluxant prince—ain't love grand? Richard Lebeaux thinks that for love and companionship Thoreau turned to nature, preferring to "fall in love with the moon and the night, and find love . . . requited." I suppose there come times in the course of romance when most of us might concede that H.T. had the right idea.

In our time, however, we may have to learn to live without even nature's affections, and recognize that her love can no longer be unconditional—it's a small planet and our inamorata simply has too many suitors. Speaking for the Cape, the writer and naturalist Robert Finch has pointed out that "it is becoming more and more necessary to cut ourselves off from direct and unfettered contact with the environment that we love," adding a plea that we "restrain our numbers and demands on the land."

Unfortunately, I doubt that many will heed Finch by practicing restraint and making sacrifices; abandoned gratification is not a hallmark of our post-industrialist society. Who among us is prepared to deny ourselves the pleasures of the still-comely Cape? To forsake that cunning cottage, priced to sell? The Cape's popularity has not yet peaked and people keep coming, and worse, staying—what modern man desires he simply must and will possess. The first generation willing to settle for an arm's length, platonic relationship with Cape Cod has not yet been born.

When my father was a young man struggling up from the Depression's poverty, it was considered an extraordinary privilege to be able to afford a week's rental of a Cape cottage. Later, as the generation that fought in World War II aged and prospered, an entire summer's stay came within reach, with some becoming well enough off to build or buy. Today, many of my Baby Boom peers already have second homes on the Cape. When the Cape real estate market went bust in the early 1990s, some predicted it would take at least a decade to recover, but this is Cape Cod we're talking about—with bargains galore housing sales bounced back almost immediately, and it's likely that the Cape will continue to grow steadily if not exponentially in the near future.

Given all that, the Cape's future as a unique "place apart" is not totally bleak. More and more property is coming under public or private conservancy, a means of preservation Thoreau encouraged, and some of the Cape's best parts, its most defining features, are untouchable for perpetuity. Driving from the Old King's Highway through the National Seashore to Provincetown, for instance, you run into lots of summer traffic but little in the way of large-scale development. The route I've outlined is not just a sort of extended Potemkin village in reverse, an uncluttered bit of the old Cape masking the reality of new Cape density; in fact, it represents a significant swath of the peninsula. Unquestionably there are parts of the Cape that now resemble Boston suburbs, and more will no doubt follow, but with fingers crossed I opine that the Cape's historic and natural character will never be fully compromised, especially if the Cape Cod Commission lives up to its promise. Perhaps that view will strike some as too panglossian, and it may well be; the heart and mind rebel at more pessimistic scenarios. Thoughts of my beautiful Cape changed utterly are too terrible to bear.

The damp fall air, some wine from the bar, journey's end—all had put me in a reflective mood; some valedictory thoughts seemed in order, and they moved through my mind as steadily as the *Provincetown II* cut through mounting swells.

Even before venturing out, I had expected that walking the Great Beach would leave a large imprint on my soul, and the prophecy had been fulfilled. Elements of self were not the least of what I discovered, or rediscovered, on Thoreau's Cape Cod; I observed that I retained powers of observation, got a clear sense that my senses remained acute and alive, and was able to take huge pleasure in an ability to be pleased by the smallest things. If the best we can hope for in life or in any venture is improvement on the margins, then by that measure my Cape sojourn had been an unqualified success.

But I was also in search of some deeper meaning, something that went beyond the marginal. Thoreau went out to Walden "to live deliberately, to front only the essential facts of life . . . and not, when I came to die, discover that I had not lived." A similar impulse had been among my ulterior motives for seeking succor and solitude along the Great Beach. I knew I was starting to harden a bit, becoming more and more set in my ways and prone to bouts of cynicism, that bitter distillate of disappointment and dashed hopes. Still, I had always struggled to keep up faith and good humor in the face of absurdity, and I was inspired by Thoreau's belief that we are infinitely capable of reaching higher. And so, though it was little more than an extended stint of stopping to smell the salt spray roses, I hoped that my simple excursion across Thoreau's Cape Cod might provide me with some direction as to how to make the second half of my life more purposeful and fulfilling than the first, and I wondered if the Great Beach held any answers.

Alas, no definitive answers were yielded up, I must report, no great revelations, no insights that came to me in a burst of epiphany—but I did get hints and clues to a better way, which I continue to puzzle out. After spending long hours walking alone on the beach, I could swear that a sea change had taken place within me, palpable as it was near to indescribable. There was little question that my perspective had been expanded, my priorities reordered. During and following the walk I felt cleansed, keener-eyed, with a sharper sense of what's important for living and what's not. The very air was a tonic, and I was filled with a peace and serenity I'd yearned for but never known. Being closer to nature than I'd ever been before, I experienced not so much a spiritual awakening (for I don't believe my spirit had been nap-ping) as a diminishing interest in things materialistic. Mammon and his modern values were conspicuous by their absence during my walk; there are no monuments erected to that false god in the true Atlantic City.

The journey along the Outer Cape had also been enjoyable, even *fun*, despite a few moments of physical discomfort. If I could have arranged it, I'd be out there still, walking back and forth, Eastham to Provincetown, Provincetown to Eastham, wearing a path in the sand carpet. But just as Thoreau knew at some point that it was time for him to leave Walden woods, I knew it was time for me to return to Boston. H.T.'s famous friend and neigh-bor, Ralph Waldo Emerson, remarked, "What lies behind us and what lies before us are small matters compared to what lies within us." (A bit of a bromide, yes, but still, an Emersonian bromide.) The challenge as I saw it was to bring values gleaned from the Great Beach along on my ongoing inner journey as well as back with me to life in the urban jungle. I knew retaining the spirit of the beach walk would not be easy—"Simplicity! Simplicity! Simplicity!" H.T. wrote, but simplicity, I think, is the hardest thing to achieve.

We were now out in mid-bay, halfway to Boston. A lone cormo-rant passed over the bow, wings working furiously. I thought it an unusual sighting and checked my book, which confirmed that cormorants prefer near-shore rocks and pilings. There was a real sense of *urgency* to his Provincetown-bound flight, as if he had read the same book.

With the aid of conspiring skies, darkness had come seemingly ahead of schedule; didn't Yogi Berra once say something like "It gets late early around here?" Soon Minot Light showed itself, but barely. I wouldn't want to have been a sailor dependent on Minot for guidance this night, as its lantern was hardly brighter than a flashlight working on dying batteries. As always when passing this point, I shivered involuntarily, perhaps recalling the dead — the two Minot keepers swept to a lonely, icy end during the great gale of 1851, and the Irish immigrants lost at nearby Cohasset in 1849. Tonight I also remembered my own departed father and brother, for our family had once spent a happy, carefree summer at Minot Beach that even Scituate's hypothermic seas couldn't ruin. It was not our last summer together by any means, but it might have been the last season when we were all of us young together.

As the lighthouse receded, I ruminated upon Thoreau's final visit to the Cape in 1857, the account of which he set down in his journal. The biggest change from 1849 was the relative speed and dependability of his transportation: on June 22 he left Provincetown on a 9 A.M. steamer to Boston, caught a train in the capital, and was back in Concord by late afternoon. This was quite a contrast to the opening of his original jaunt, which reads like Crusaders trying to get to the Holy Land.

The 1857 journal entry is not included in most editions of *Cape Cod* presently available at bookstores, but it came appended to the 1951 W. W. Norton printing that had so moved me one dark and stormy night. For most modern readers *Cape Cod* concludes with the famous line "A man may stand there and put all America behind him," but for those whose copies contain the journal as epilogue, the last sentence is "Get home at 5 P.M."

"*Get home at 5 P.M.*" These final words in his journal are the simple, brief coda to Henry David Thoreau's great Cape Cod writings. Considering that it was written by a traveling man in his prime who would be dead in less than five years, this mundane entry, to me, strikes an almost elegiac note. On that June day could H.T. have had any inkling that he'd never see the Cape, a place he'd come to love, again? What plans for future trips did the onset of his fatal bout with tuberculosis disrupt? I know the last words of the man who had also explored the Maine woods were "moose" and "Indian," but as he lay dying, did he close his eyes and dream of a heaven of sand as well?

When Thoreau made his ultimate journey to a shore further west at age forty-four, he did so with "pleasure and peace," said one deathbed attendant. Clearly he had lived life as he saw fit, on his terms, and he passed on with little remorse. Be that as it may, I still can't help wondering if H.T. was at all disappointed that he never held a bound copy of *Cape Cod* in his hands, never got the chance to place it alongside *Walden* on his library shelves. Drawn on for lecture materials in the early 1850s, later serialized in part in *Putnam's Monthly Magazine*, tinkered with off and on over the years by the author, *Cape Cod*'s manuscript was edited to completion by Ellery Channing and Thoreau's sister Sophia after his death in 1862. H.T. set out to "make a book on Cape Cod," and produced a masterful one, but it was published as such only posthumously.

The *Provincetown II* had stolen past the harbor islands and was soon hard by Castle Island. The shining city on a hill was strangely darkened, as if it had been hit by a blackout, not a bulb showing in any of the skyscrapers—who had hid the lights?

It would have been easy to let Boston's grave, unwelcoming countenance and the ghostly October air infect me with melancholy and regret, but as we moved through the inner harbor I instead felt curiously sanguine, even ecstatic. How different life's landscape appears when you have a goal to reach, when your journey seems to be leading in the direction of your dreams. For a moment I saw myself on the beach again, rounding a point, and I felt as if I might be on the verge of beholding a grand view just ahead. Yes, I'd had this feeling before; maybe this time it would hold. But this time it also came attached with a cautionary note, for somewhere along the way I'd been stripped of the young man's last great stubborn delusion, that there will always be time enough for everything.

We docked at South Boston on time, 6:30 P.M., and I walked to South Station to catch a train. Out of habit I was about to stop in at Clarke's, my favorite watering hole, then hesitated. I had a story to tell, but not to those perched on barstools. Something of the lonely cormorant's flight had taken hold of me; I could almost feel the hastening beat of its wings reverberate in my breast, and I knew I'd not yet reached my true destination, which had to do with the writing of a book. I kept walking through the terminal and boarded a train, thinking all the while about time and tide and how, if you don't keep close watch on their flow, someone else might get to finish your manuscript, or worse, dictate your epitaph.

Got home at 8 P.M.

Index of Place Names